Plug Nickel

Shoestring Boat Restoration:
How I Turned an Old Fiberglass Boat Mold
into a Beautiful Wooden Sailboat, and
What I Learned Along the Way

volume one

BY JOEL THURTELL

Hardalee Press

Copyright © by Joel Thurtell

Published by Hardalee Press
11803 Priscilla Lane
Plymouth, MI 48170

All rights reserved. Printed in the United States of America. No part of this books may be reproduced in any manner whatsoever without written permission except in the case of brief quotations embodied in critical articles and reviews. For information, address Hardalee Press, 11803 Priscilla lane, Plymouth, MI 48170.

All photos are by Joel Thurtell unless otherwise indicated
Cover design by Maya Rhodes
Interior design by Peggy Castine

Library of Congress Control Number: 2009906578

Thurtell, Joel Howard

ISBN 978-0-9759969-2-8

Dedication

*This book is for my wife,
Karen Fonde,
whose candid advice
helped me focus.*

TABLE OF CONTENTS

The Last Wooden Nickel 1
The Last Wooden Nickel, Part 2 5
The Last Wooden Nickel, Part 3 9
Ghost Boat 12
Subversive Idea 16
A Big Deal 20
Cedar & Spruce, et al. 24
The Lingo of Lightnings 28
Be Seated, Please 32
Tape Rule 37
Fear of Drilling 40
Anatomy of a Screw-Up 45
Side Show 51
My First Boat 58
Numbers Game 64
Boom Time 68
Plug It In 72
The Caretaker 76
Maybe 82
The Pessimist 87

PREFACE TO THE SECOND EDITION

Bob Astrove's first e-mail came in early 2009. The gist of it was that my columns in the International Lightning Class Association's publication, "The Flashes," had inspired aficionados of wooden Lightnings to convene a yearly regatta for woodies at Lake Onondaga in upstate new York. Though my Flashes columns were the sparkplug, he said, I had never put in an appearance at the annual woodie conclave. He wished I would try to attend the next one in July 2009.

It was winter when Bob's e-mail arrived, and I was more focused on clearing snow off my driveway than sailing. But the seed was planted. I recalled the last time I hitched the trailer to my car and pulled my wooden Lightning, Plug Nickel, out East. The destination in 2001 was Mystic Seaport and the Designers Recognition Rendezvous honoring naval architects Drake Sparkman and Olin Stephens. Among many other accomplishments, Sparkman and Stephens in 1938 produced plans for our cherished Lightning.

Lightning Number One was built at nearby Skaneateles, as were many succeeding Lightnings, and in those early days all were made of wood. Along with my Plug Nickel at Mystic Seaport, we got to see that original Lightning Number One, brought to the show by its owner, Jack Ryan, and sold that weekend to the ILCA.

Along with my boat, Plug Nickel, I packed a small box of fifty copies of a little book I'd just published. It was called "Plug Nickel." The book was a compilation of my first 17 Flashes columns. I'd planned on selling the books at Mystic, but found the event so fascinating that I forgot about my little commercial venture.

When Bob Astrove mentioned the 2009 wooden Lightning get-together to me, I began thinking about my former grandiose plan to publish all of my Flashes columns – some 55 or more of them over five and a half years. Eventually, I settled on a less-ambitious plan – to re-publish the original collection plus three columns – a round twenty articles – as Volume One, with the idea of following it with another twenty or so columns in a later Volume Two and finally topping the effort with Volume Three, thus putting into print all of my wooden Lightning columns.

So this is the plan: Go to the Lake Onondaga meet in July 2009, taking both Plug Nickels with me, sailboat and book. Last time, the book was run off on a friend's photocopier. This time, it is commercially printed in a perfect-bound paperback cover with a new front and back design and the text has been re-set.

I'm hoping I'll come home with enough ideas for future columns to kick-start Volume Four.

–Joel Thurtell, Plymouth, Michigan, June 2009

INTRODUCTION

Plug Nickel was a boat before it was a book. But before there could be a boat, there had to be an obsession. This book, "Plug Nickel," is about the obsession that finally, after nearly seven years, launched the boat called Plug Nickel.

Without the obsession, the boat would not have been possible.

Before the obsession, there was a fantasy. And the fantasy was based on a rumor.

Seven years ago, I heard about a hull then in storage at Nickels Boat Works in Fenton, Mich. The story went that, in 1965, the Nickels & Holman Boat Co. in Fenton stopped production of wooden boats and switched to the new material called fiber glass. But to manufacture glass boats, the company needed to build one last woodie. This hull would be used as a male mold, or "plug," for making plastic Lightnings.

The plug was thus an artifact that symbolized the boatbuilding industry's rejection of traditional wood manufacturing techniques as it turned to this new artificial material. This bare hull, then, embodied a whole change in technology, at least as it occurred in one boatyard.

Built by Dave Nickels, it was literally the last wooden nickel, except for a handful of custom-ordered woodies.

That there was a boat created specifically to move this one company out of the wood age fascinated me. The idea of turning this hull, which its makers considered no more than a tool, into a sailable boat captured my imagination.

It seemed like a simple idea, really. The hull was already there. Put a mast and boom on it, find a rudder and centerboard and the rest should be easy.

"Plug Nickel," the book, tells why it's not so easy turning a symbol into a boat.

The book is a collection of columns I've written for the Flashes, the newsletter of the International Lightning Class Association.

It's thanks to Flashes Editor Karen Johnson that I began writing the columns in the fall of 1999. She had the confidence that I could do it, even though I had my doubts.

Others who understood the potential of this conglomeration of mahogany and cedar were veteran Lightning sailor Bob Mathers, who encouraged me throughout this long project, and Wylie Gerdes, my sailing buddy and the onetime Detroit Free Press sailing writer.

Dave Nickels of Nickels Boat Works, the man who built the plug in 1965, was always patient and ready to answer my many questions as I forged ahead with what seemed like an endless project.

At a critical point, boatbuilder Hugh Horton steered me to another boatbuilder, Ron Sell, who breathed life and color into the old plug.

Peggy Castine continued to see the possibility of a book when I had lost faith in the Plug's literary potential.

My wife, Karen Fonde and my sons, Adam and Abe, were patient with me even though it meant I was spending long hours with a boat rather than with them, only to return and regale them with intricate descriptions of my latest wooden boat problems.

I want to thank readers of the Flashes, whose e-mails and comments have encouraged me to keep cranking out the wooden boat columns.

There will be more, I promise.

The story of Plug Nickel sails on.

– Joel Thurtell, Plymouth, Michigan, June 2001

THE LAST WOODEN NICKEL

My first Lightning was a 1970s Nickels & Holman boat which turned out to be a bit heavy with waterlogged foam. Newer boats supposedly used a superior foam which was not as prone to water saturation, I was assured. But I decided the ultimate solution was to have a boat that didn't use foam at all. A wooden boat.

First sight of Plug in Nickels Boat Works shed 11-15-94

The idea of owning a wooden Lightning became a driving force for me when I learned of a 1953 Nickels & Holman Lightning for sale in Lansing, Mich. The idea took on more urgency when I learned the price: Boat, trailer, sails, all for $400. One catch — the aluminum mast was broken.

Hey, so what? Never one to let such obvious detractions get in the way of my obsessive need to increase my list of projects, I drove over to Lansing for a look. I liked what I saw. The boat, #5885, had been dry-sailed for years and the hull was in great shape. So what if the deck canvas appeared in need of replacement? Big deal. What's one chore more or less? And there were two – TWO! – centerboards in the deal, plus a neat mahogany kick-up rudder. The broken mast seemed hardly to matter. Truly, the seller didn't need to make a pitch. I did all the persuading myself, paid the man $400 and hitched the trailer to

Taking a closer look outside

my car. That was in mid-summer 1993.

Looking back, it doesn't seem like such a bad deal. For under $300 I had the mast welded back together, so that with the cost of boat and trailer licenses I had about $700 invested in a smooth sailing wooden Lightning. I should have been happy.

I WAS happy. I recall the first time I sailed 5885. In the 1980s, I had restored two wooden Snipes, but for several years I'd been sailing fiberglass boats. I'd forgotten what a wooden boat sounds like. A fiberglass Lightning has a fair amount of plastic and foam between water and crew. It never occurred to me that all that plastic and foam is a good sound insulator until the first time I got underway on Cass Lake and heard water running under my wood-planked hull. I loved that sound. In the glass boat, that rushing-over-the-water feeling was missing, and I never knew the pleasure of hearing my boat until I sailed the woody.

I sold my glass Lightning and entered the summer of 1994 with 5885, the last in a series of boats christened "Maybe." We had lots of fun in that boat, including a glorious capsize in 30 mph winds on Douglas Lake which my family still talks about whenever the subject of high winds, my general incompetence or lost glasses comes up.

But that was the summer when I heard the rumor about the plug. A fellow member of the Pontiac Yacht Club, Tom Watkins, is a woodworker and wooden boat fancier. One day at the club, Tom told me of a wooden Lightning he'd discovered. The last wooden Lightning built by Nickels & Holman. Built in fall 1965 by none other than Dave Nickels.

The last wooden Nickel, you might say.

Built as a true Nickels & Holman Lightning, this hull was never launched, never sold. By the mid-1960s, Nickels & Holman realized that the market had shifted. Customers no longer wanted high-maintenance wooden boats. They wanted low-upkeep boats. That meant fiberglass. So instead of selling the last wooden boat, Nickels & Holman used it as a male plug for making female molds. This hull, therefore, is the progenitor of the fiberglass Lightnings made by Nickels & Holman. The pappy of them all.

What's more, from a practical standpoint, here was a true wooden Lightning with a fiberglass skin on hull and yes, even the deck, because the plug had been used for making deck molds, too. For a mere $500, here was a boat that lacked only hardware, mast, boom and sails.

Wow! Now I looked at my old 5885, much in need of a new canvas deck cover. To have a wooden boat with a smart, protective fiberglass skin. Sounded too good to be true.

Amazing what a little water and a sponge will do - mahogany centerboard trunk, mahogany frames, western red cedar planks. There is hope!

And it was, at least for me. Because Tom Watkins had dibs on it. He was going to buy it and put it on the lake and have the prettiest wooden boat at PYC, he said.

Dave Nickels had even suggested a name, Tom said. "Plug Nickel."

So much for that idea.

But I couldn't stop thinking about it. Finally, in November 1994, I called Dave Nickels about another matter and brought up the plug.

"It's still here," Dave said. "Tom came and looked at it, he said he'd buy it, but he never came back."

"Okay," I said. "I'll be up soon."

It never occurred to me to wonder why Tom Watkins, a skilled woodworker, didn't buy the plug.

Instead, I arranged a day off from work and drove to Fenton. Dave said his brother, George, would handle the deal. George and I walked behind the Nickels Boat Works building, formerly the home of the now-defunct Nickels & Holman firm that paid Dave to build the plug. There is a shed out back with a metal roof and open sides. In it lay a damaged Finn-class sailboat, a long wooden sailboat of no special interest and there, yes, upside down, there it was: The glass-and-polyester skin was smooth and shiny –so shiny it reflected light and images. A Lightning!

Hmmm. Wait a minute. I could see hairline cracks and, well, some cracks that were more than a hair or two wide. One area at the stern was missing plastic entirely. That was good, I thought, because it showed me that the skin was fairly thin. It would give protection, but not be too heavy.

I switched a flashlight on and crawled under the boat. What I saw amazed me. Despite dust, the centerboard trunk shone. Varnish on the western red cedar planks and mahogany frames was still smooth, albeit dusty. Doggone, this IS a boat, I thought.

I looked again at the cracks on the hull. No big deal, that can be filled, I thought.

Back in the office, I wrote a check.

On a piece of torn note paper, George Nickels scrawled, "Sold one lightning 'wood' to Joel Thurtell for $500 – George Nickels, 11-15-94."

Let's see, I thought, if I do this, I'll need a mast, a boom, a centerboard, a bucket of hardware, sails, a trailer and some pretty epoxy paint.

No big deal.

And, oh yes, a place to work on the boat.

Minor details . . .

THE LAST WOODEN NICKEL PART 2
Or, A Dumb-Ass Idea

I was high all the way home from Fenton that day in November 1994 when I bought the last wooden Nickels hull. I was still excited that evening as my wife, Karen Fonde, and I cooked dinner. I told Karen what I'd done. She suppressed her excitement.

No going back: The Plug five minutes after I started blasting the glass with a heat gun.

"I'm going to call it Plug Nickel," I said.

"I call it a dumb-ass idea!" Karen said.

There have been times – many times – when I thought her name was the best one for this project.

But in 1994 I was planning for the next summer. Plug Nickel would be my sailboat that year. Dave and George Nickels had offered to store the plug until I could pick it up in spring 1995. Meanwhile, I sold 5885 to Tom Watkins, the guy who originally planned to buy and restore the plug. By then I had also sold my first Lightning, a glass boat. Because I acquired two centerboards with 5885, I did some board juggling and wound up with a stainless centerboard for the plug. I also sold 5885 minus trailer, so that gave me a heavy Nickels & Holman trailer. And I kept the

Side view of Plug in my shop circa 1996. Note numerous areas where I've filled splinters and splits with epoxy resin.

homebuilt kick-up rudder from 5885 because we sail in the shoal waters of Georgian Bay where a fixed rudder is an invitation for disaster.

I ran an ad in the ILCA Lightning Flashes newsletter asking for Lightning parts and eventually bought not one but two nice Bryant aluminum masts, a box or two of hardware, various sails, rudders, spinnaker poles and an entire set of wooden Lightning frames, stem and transom from someone who dismantled a boat. I even acquired a full set of Lightning blueprints.

What I lacked was a good place to work on the boat.

At first, that didn't seem like a problem. That's because I estimated I'd have the boat ready for water in a few weeks.

In early 1995 Dave Nickels hoisted the hull onto 5885's old trailer. For a few minutes before departing for home in Plymouth, I stood by the plug chatting with Dave. It's a conversation I remember vividly and often.

"Dave," I said, "If this were your boat, what would you do with it?"

"First I'd take all that #@!# off the hull," Dave said. He was talking about the fiberglass and resin skin added by Nickels & Holman to make the desired hull shape as well as a slick surface for removing molds.

"I'd remove all of that, cover the hull with West System epoxy and paint it," Dave said. "That's what we did with the wooden Nickels & Holman boats."

What to do with the boat's skin had been a topic of conversation over lunch at the Fenton Burger King that day. George and Dave saw disadvantages to keeping the skin. Mainly, there was a danger that rot would set into the wood if water ever got trapped between the plastic skin and the wooden planks.

Like all later wooden Nickels & Holman hulls, this boat was single-planked with western red cedar planks glued together. The glued planks plus a good epoxy surface should make a watertight boat, Dave said.

This talk gave me something more than a Whopper to digest. One of the big selling points for this boat was the fact that it had this smooth, shiny fiberglass skin. Take it off? That smacked of heresy.

I called Gougeon Brothers. One of their epoxy experts agreed that repairing the old skin might be asking for problems. Why not remove it? Use a heat gun and a scraper and it will come right off, he said. Then, contrary to the Nickels Brothers, he suggested once the skin was off that I should replace it with fiberglass and West System epoxy.

I had a choice: I could patch the old skin, install hardware and go sailing. Or I could remove the skin, make a decision about replacement of fiberglass later, but have the boat in the water later in the summer.

I decided to take the expert's advice. I bought a heat gun and a scraper and in my garage, wearing a mask, I began the stinky, hot task of removing plastic and fiberglass from the sides and transom. After several hours altogether of now and then work on the project, I had removed all the plastic from those parts. But I also found that splinters of cedar were coming off, too. When I finished removing the plastic, I went around the boat filling the splinter holes with thickened epoxy, then sanding it down.

At some point that summer, I realized that the plug would not be ready for sailing that year. At Pontiac Yacht Club I found a 1970s Eichenlaub for sale: $1,050 for boat, trailer, sails. I named it Meantime because I planned to keep it only a short time, until the plug was ready.

That was 1995. It is now late summer 1999. I am still sailing in Meantime.

THE LAST WOODEN NICKEL PART 3
Or, That Sinking Feeling

I'll never forget the moment I set down the heat gun, removed my breathing mask and goggles, stood back and looked at the first segment of fiberglass and plastic I scraped off Plug Nickel. Until that instant, I had a smooth, tough hull, although it had various flaws. Now, I realized, I no longer had a choice about removing the skin. I had so damaged it that repair would be costly if it was even possible. I had to finish the job of removing fiberglass and resin.

It was a sinking feeling. I really felt depressed. There was no going back. The idea I had sold myself – of restoring a wooden Lightning that had never been sailed, one that already had a fiberglass skin – was dead. This boat, if it ever became a boat, would be one with a new surface of some kind.

So I went ahead with the heat gun and scraper, but with less excitement and more worry about what damage I might do to the hull.

That fiberglass skin had served as the foundation for a whole set of decisions about this boat. The idea that the shape of this boat – thanks to the fiberglass – was a MODERN hull shape made me decide to rig the boat as a modern boat, rather than as a classic or historic boat of the mid-1960s. This boat's hull would be the same as the latest Nickels & Holman boats, built in 1996. The entire rig would be the latest, greatest.

But now I was on my way back to the original Nickels & Holman hull shape. At the time, it never occurred to me that I might rethink the rigging decision. I was too caught up, too concerned about the removal of "all that #@!#."

The year 1995 was the beginning of great upheaval for me. I was and again am a reporter on the Detroit Free Press. But on July 13, 1995 my union – The Newspaper Guild – struck along

> There was no going back. The idea I had sold myself – of restoring a wooden Lightning that had never been sailed, one that already had a fiberglass skin – was dead. This boat, if it ever became a boat, would be one with a new surface of some kind.

with several other unions against the Detroit News and Detroit Free Press. I was out of a job and busy starting a business, trying to create a new job. Meanwhile, realizing the plug project was going to take a long time, I rented some storage space and mothballed the hull.

Roughly a year later, I rented warehouse space for my business. The place had room for the Lightning. During the winter of 1996-97 I got back to work. I sanded lightly and revarnished the interior. I put a primer coat of paint on the deck. I flipped the boat and began removing the skin from the bottom.

Now I ran into serious problems. It turned out that the plastic bottom varied from roughly an eighth of an inch thick at the stern to an inch and a half thick near the forward area around the centerboard trunk. At the stern, where some plastic was missing, I'd led myself to believe that taking this stuff off would be a cinch. But as the plastic became thicker, I found the heat gun would not work. I tried a compressed air chisel. Marginal. Hammer and chisel worked, but it was slow. And occasionally, I made deep gouges in the hull planks.

Very depressing.

Enter Hugh Horton. Hugh is a Detroit area boat builder who specializes in sailing canoes, so-called 50-50 boats because you paddle half the time and sail the other half. I met Hugh in a book club run by a mutual friend at the Free Press. Hugh looked over my hull and gave me some advice about fixing it. Then he mentioned the name of his friend, Ron Sell, of Unadilla Boat Works near Dexter, Mich. Ron does boat repairs.

Lacking time and expertise to finish the job, I hired Ron. He cut and glued pieces of wood to plug my grossest fiberglass removal errors. He faired the hull. He laid down a skin of fiberglass and West System epoxy. That was as far as he got by fall 1998.

Early in the summer of 1999, Ron finished the hull and deck with a pretty two-tone coating of paint. Now Plug Nickel is at Nickels Boat Works once again, waiting for hardware and rigging.

I don't regret having removed all that plastic. I estimate I took well over 100 pounds of material off the hull. According to Dave Nickels, the best Nickels & Holman glass boats were the early ones made from this plug between 1966-74. Those were fast boats, better than later attempts at reshaping the hull, Dave says.

As for the rig, there is no question about having a modern rig. We don't race. We sail for fun. But we like the rig to be convenient and that means a modern rig with aluminum mast.

Right now, I'm waiting for Dave Nickels to install hardware. He says it will be ready in September 1999. Perhaps I will launch Plug Nickel before the year 2000.

But it doesn't matter. On the hoist at Pontiac Yacht Club I have Meantime, the venerable glass boat that has served us while we wait for the wooden boat of my dreams.

GHOST BOAT

In my attic, there is a skeleton. If my wife only knew. It's the mortal remains of a boat. A wooden Lightning sailboat all cramped under the rafters of our garage loft. I don't talk about it much. Certainly not in Karen's presence. The number of boats in my inventory is a sore subject around here.

The fact that I can speak of an "inventory" is a measure of the problem.

Not that I see it as a problem.

Once a few years ago, I overheard Karen talking on the phone with her brother. She was joking about the number of boats I owned. I was lurking in the basement family room, hearing it all. There was the Chris-Craft. True. There was the fiberglass Lightning. Correct. The wooden Lightning plug. Right. But wait a minute – she had the count up to three – <u>three</u> – Lightnings. Where was the third?

Then I remembered. In a basement cupboard, incomplete, lies the hull of a 19-inch scale model of a Lightning. The model is part of the inventory, too. Absolutely.

Okay, I can accept that.

But please don't tell her about the Lightning in the garage loft.

And by the way, since that count was made, I've acquired one, two, no really three Sunfish. Or Sunfishes. (Anybody know the plural of Sunfish?)

It happened this way. After I bought the wooden Lightning plug from the Nickels brothers for $500, I decided the cheap way to outfit the boat would be to search for second-hand parts such as mast, boom, hardware, rudder, sails, etc. So I ran an ad in the International Lightning Class Association newsletter, the Flashes. I let the world know that I was in the market for everything to do with Lightnings.

That's how I located not one but two nice oval aluminum Bryant masts in Kansas. Had them trucked to my house in Plymouth, Mich. I got calls from all over the country offering me

Lightning parts, but one offer really surprised me.

It came from Canton, Mich., just a stone's throw down the road from me. The seller identified himself as John Bray, and immediately I had a mental image: a color picture of a donkey. The Bray family coat of arms might as well be a jackass rampant on a field of hamburgers and onions. The Brays own a famous little diner in Westland, Mich. It's one of these places with round stools at a counter and cheap burgers. The original fast food joint. And outside the store, on a pedestal, there truly is a life-size statue of a black donkey standing on its hind legs pawing the air.

So the owner of this place is calling me to say he has a 1954 Nickels & Holman Lightning he'd like me to buy. And where is it stored? Why, in a garage behind that pawing burro.

One catch: The boat, he said, has been, shall we say, dismantled.

Dismantled?

As in taken apart?

But why would anyone do that?

His plan was to rebuild the boat from stem to stern, he said. But once he had removed the planks from bottom and sides, creating a big pile of used lumber, he lost steam for the project. The whole kit and kaboodle was sitting in the garage behind his hamburger stand – boat (in pieces), wooden mast, hardware, trailer, rudder. The works. Sails were at his house. Now that I think of it, there was no boom or centerboard. Anyway, for $350 I could have the works, he said.

I gave it some thought.

Let's pause for a moment now. Let's reflect on what I just said.

The guy has a "dismantled" Lightning, i.e., a Lightning that most likely never will sail again. Which would cost a ton of money and time to restore. And he wants to SELL it? My God, what an absurd proposition.

But even worse, I stopped to THINK about it!

What is wrong here?

Having pondered John Bray's generous offer, I made a phone call. Believe it or not, I found a buyer for the trailer and wooden mast. Both for $350. I got rid of the hardest things to store and acquired a mess of Lightning parts for nothing beyond the trouble of carting it away. I declined to take the planks for lack of a space to keep them. But the other pieces – rudder, sails, a box of somewhat worn silicon bronze screws and some pieces of antique sailing hardware became mine.

As well as the frames.

The stem.

And the transom, which has the words "Plymouth, Mich." painted on it.

And that's where it came to rest, in an attic in Plymouth.

What a lucky guy I am.

Along with the parts, John Bray gave me a set of blueprints and the official ILCA measurement certificate for Yacht Number 5602. It says the first owner was Harold Muntz of Hickory Corners, Mich.

At some point, it appears that I admitted owning this ghost of a boat and my name was published in the Lightning Yearbook alongside its number. Fearing word of this indiscretion would somehow filter back to my home and hearth, I called Karen Johnson at the ILCA and explained the state of Lightning 5602.

"I'll put it down as 'destroyed,'" she said.

Sure enough, next to 5602 in the Yearbook directory now stands this stark description: "Boat Destroyed."

It has an awful, final ring to it.

Next to those grim words there is a little x.

As if the boat received a Christian burial.

Which, of course, it did not, since it's resting a good 10 feet off the ground, hidden behind a pile of old 2-by-4s.

Question: What happens when we move? Will my grave little secret come tumbling down to roost on the garage floor?

Will I be ordered to send this ridiculous collection to the landfill?

Or will I have sense enough to spirit it to a better, more final resting place?

Something tells me we have not heard the last of 5602.

I haven't mentioned the idea I harbor late at night.

It involves a few pieces of plywood – marine grade, of course. I believe what I'm dreaming of has a name.

"Resurrection."

That would fit nicely on the transom, wouldn't it?

SUBVERSIVE IDEA

How many Lightning operators would be willing to break the law? No, I'm not talking about the speed limit. It's 50 m.p.h. on Cass Lake, where I do most of my sailing. I may be a dreamer, but I'm not crazy.

I'm talking about the rule that says a Lightning's rudder must be a rigid steering device.

You can legally race with any rudder that doesn't stick down into the water a couple feet asking for shoals and sandbars and beaches and sunken logs to grab it. Definitely a design defect, in my humble opinion.

What can we do about it?

Well, I am not a revolutionary. I don't expect the rules to change.

But outside of racing, there is a real option in the matter of fixed rudders.

Why am I concerned about rudders?

I chose to sail Lightnings 10 or 15 years ago, after my 470 proved too small and tippy for our family of four. The Lightning cockpit has lots of room, the boat is fast, maneuverable and fun to sail. We also believed it would be harder to capsize than a 470, which is true. But capsizes, or "capsizion," as my younger son Abe calls it, is another column.

I bought a Lightning, an old glass boat that was waterlogged, as it turned out, but members of my wife's family immediately pointed to a design defect –- that rigid rudder. It was great that the centerboard would swing up if it struck something hard, but that rudder looked dangerous.

In the Georgian Bay, where we spend our summer vacations, the ground above and below water is solid rock. Everything capable of being stood on, it seems, is good, hard granite. Even in high water times, granite shoals are a major hazard to boats. Last summer, with water near an all-time low, we saw ugly yellow patches of water revealing shoals we never knew about. This

The kick-up rudder looks a lot like a regular rudder when down, but kicks up to allow the boat to sail safely in shallow waters.

Photo by Karen Fonde

year, predictions are coming in that we'll have a foot less water compared to last year, so we'll be drawing up entirely new mental maps of our boating waters.

Now, when cruising in a boat with appendages that dangle underwater, be they lower units of outboard motors, centerboards or rudders, there is a risk of serious damage if you collide with a shoal. I've been in boats when this happened, and it's not something I'd want to happen in a boat with a sail full of wind. The cursing alone could get you jailed in some parts of Michigan.

If a rudder drags against a sandbar, shoal, tree stump or other object with a mind to stay where it is, the least that may happen is the rudder will spring the gudgeons out of the transom. Then you can practice steering by trimming the sails.

The danger is one issue. Convenience is another. Ever been cruising along a beach and had to struggle to remove the rudder before making a landfall? If you don't get that rudder out in time, you can hurt your boat. Or simply come to a standstill where you don't want to be. It's a pain.

The problem was solved for me the day I bought Lightning 5885 from a fellow who had built a new rudder capable of swinging up and out of harm's way. It's rather simple. Instead of being a fixed plate sandwiched between two pieces of wood, the rudder is connected to the two "sandwich" boards by a bolt. There is a metal loop at the straight forward edge of the rudder just before it curves underwater. Hooked to that loop is a small line which runs up the rudder to a block at the corner made by the rudder and tiller. The line leads through that block, making a roughly right-angle bend and continues underneath the tiller to a cleat. When the rope is pulled taut and cleated, the rudder will stay in its normal down position for steering. But when the line is uncleated, tension on the rudder is gone and the rudder floats to the surface. When it is floating, the rudder still is capable of steering the boat, though not very well. However, the important point is that it is then in line with the bottom of the hull and not likely to snag on anything that could cause trouble.

I took 5885 to Canada. I never struck a shoal, but I was comforted by the idea that if I hit bottom, my centerboard, also on a hinge, would move rather than tear at the boat's bottom. And my rudder would literally not be a drag. When I sold 5885, I kept that kick-up rudder. To this day, the kick-up is my rudder of choice, no matter what boat I'm sailing.

I've been told that I could probably race with this rudder at the Pontiac Yacht Club, but might hear some challenges if I tried it elsewhere or at a district race. Since I'm not a racer, it doesn't really matter.

It's probably well that the kick-up is illegal in racing, because anyone with a swinging rudder would enjoy an advantage. I was in a race once in which several boats sailed over a sandbar and crews wound up perched on the bows, trying to prop the sterns up and clear the rudder in the shallow water. The tactic slowed everyone down to a creep. A boat equipped with my kick-up would have cruised easily over those waters without any crew acrobatics.

For general sailing, the kick-up is great. Anything the hull will clear, the rudder will slide over.

I've considered finding a woodshop to custom make kick-up

rudders so I can offer them to cruising Lightning sailors. Another possibility would be to have blueprints made and offer plans for sale. When I priced a new wooden Lightning rudder, I learned that the cost would run to $450 or more. A custom-made kick-up likely would cost a lot more than that.

Is there any interest in a highly illegal but very rational kick-up rudder among Lightning sailors?

A BIG DEAL

Fourteen grand. That was the price – recently – of a new Lightning sailboat. Not a fiberglass boat, either. A wooden Lightning. I repeat: A wooden Lightning sold for nearly the price of a new glass boat. All by itself, that is a Big Deal.

That someone would pay roughly the same price for a wooden boat as the professional boatbuilders charge for their new-built glass boats is pretty amazing.

It shouldn't be.

After all, it costs plenty in labor and materials to build a boat, regardless of whether it's made of wood, fiberglass, or hey, whatever – aluminum, steel or concrete.

But sometime a bit after the midpoint of the last century, the people who market boats decided boat operators would be better served if hulls were made of some other material besides the material people had been using for literally millennia – wood. For sailboat construction, big or small, fiberglass emerged as the material of choice.

The primary advantage was put forth as upkeep. Meaning that with glass, there would be less or virtually no work involved in maintaining the hull. Gone would be those spring afternoons of sanding and re-varnishing brightwork on wooden hulls. And there was the longevity issue: Glass boats would not rot or otherwise deteriorate, it was supposed. (Those who have dealt with water-saturated foam in older glass boats might differ, of course.)

In any case, the market has come to deem boats made of wood to be inferior. In large part this has to do with race results. Wooden boats don't compete very well against glass boats, or at least so I hear. But then, not too many woodies race against glass boats because, so we all hear, wood doesn't fare well in those matches.

But since wooden Lightnings have not been manufactured

commercially for something like 35 years, the wooden fleet is getting pretty geriatric. How many owners of woodies have updated their rigging to competition grade?

Because the wooden portion of the fleet is old, the value of individual boats has sunk. So, when we think of wooden Lightnings, we automatically think old, outdated, slow.

How, then, did some modern boat builder manage to twist $14,000 out of a boat buyer?

The story of this boat, number 14839, is another Big Deal for all Lightning lovers, regardless of whether your preference is wood or glass. The boat was custom-designed and built for WoodenBoat magazine, and the first article of a three-part series on how the backyard builder can do it is running in WoodenBoat's current March/April 2000 issue.

The magazine commissioned boat designer Ron Smith to draw new construction plans. The original 1938 design called for a planked hull built on wooden frames. The new boat has a cold-molded bottom and plywood sides and is glued together with epoxy. It was built by professionals – Nat Bryant and Craig Picard, alumni of the Landing School of Boatbuilding and Design. The new plans are available from ILCA for $120.00.

Why is this such a big deal for everyone in the world of Lightning sailing? Because WoodenBoat magazine itself is a big deal. It's a slick, first-class publication with high-quality writing, photos and drawings. For WoodenBoat to select the Lightning class over, say, the Snipe, Thistle or Flying Scot, tells you that the Lightning class has, well, class.

Here's what WoodenBoat says: "The 19' Lightning, designed by Sparkman & Stephens, is today one of the world's most popular one-designs. Racing fleets have been established around the globe."

"Why the Lightning?" I asked WoodenBoat Editor Matthew Murphy.

"How many Lightnings have been built?" he asked me.

"About 15,000," I said.

That, pretty much, is the answer, said Murphy.

"I've been reading the Flashes for years and I've owned a

> For the Lightning to be featured, not in one issue of WoodenBoat, but in three consecutive numbers of the magazine, is a public relations bonanza. The same number of pages of advertising would cost thousands.

beat-up old Lightning and it's one of the most popular one-designs in the world. We hadn't really done anything on racing classes, and it seemed like an ideal boat, given its popularity."

For the Lightning to be featured not in one issue of WoodenBoat, but in three consecutive numbers of the magazine, is a public relations bonanza. The same number of pages of advertising would cost thousands. Flashes Editor Karen Johnson tells me ILCA can't afford to advertise in WoodenBoat. Now they don't need to.

The impact is evident already. By mid-April this year, Karen tells me, she had sold 25 sail numbers for new Lightning boats. In a normal year – a whole year – commercial builders account for the 20-25 sail numbers ILCA sells. In the first quarter, she has assigned 25 numbers, and 17 went to builders of wooden Lightnings. That's 68 percent, and it indicates a sudden interest in the Lightning by non-professionals.

It's also exciting that none of these amateur builders are ILCA members. They are new to the class.

"This is wonderful," said Johnson. While there is no reason the new woodies couldn't be raced, the people who are buying these plans are voicing a preference for day sailing and cruising, Johnson said.

This phenomenon could widen the interest in Lightnings. "There is a huge population of Lightnings that are not being raced, and we don't want to lose those boats – we're trying to get to the more general sailors," said Johnson.

For WoodenBoat's Murphy, the $14k selling price was a major feat, too.

"We had that much money into it, and I had to justify the project by getting the money back."

Justify the project? He did more than that. WoodenBoat demonstrated that a state-of-the-art wooden boat can compete in price with the commercial builders. And they showed the Lightning for what it is – a classic boat.

CEDAR & SPRUCE, ET AL.

Cement Lightnings? Over the phone, it sounded pretty neat. I was talking to a young civil engineer who was part of a team of students building a rather weird canoe. A concrete canoe.

These young people who will build our future highways and bridges were supposed to learn how to manipulate the recipe for concrete so it would float.

These concrete canoes are pretty neat, I was told. The better ones look just like commercial fiberglass canoes.

This I had to see. And forgive me, but the thought crossed my mind, "What if you made a sailboat, maybe even a Lightning, out of concrete?"

Heresy, but I was curious. I had a look at this concrete boat.

And I was far from convinced. It suddenly occurred to me that there was another reason besides learning about roadbuilding which would explain why it was civil engineers and not naval architects making boats out of cement. More than one reason, really.

It was an ugly craft. It looked like it was made – crudely made – out of Play-Doh.

They are brittle, fragile vessels. I noticed large cracks in the boat, even before it was launched. The students were handling it with utmost care, afraid that a tunk on the tarmac would bust it wide open.

I will not be building any boats, Lightning or otherwise, out of concrete.

But concrete got me reflecting about that other obstreperous building material. Fiberglass.

While big boats have been made of reinforced concrete, steel, even aluminum, with sailing dinghies it seems we come back to the old face-off between wood and fiberglass. Class rules in most cases have precluded experimentation, I suppose. I delved into the glass vs. wood debate a bit last month when I discussed WoodenBoat magazine's re-design of the Lightning. I wonder how that boat, glued together with epoxy, is holding up. Would the epoxy-encapsulated wood resist rot and prove as maintenance free as a glass boat?

Unfortunately, the magazine sold the boat and lost track of the new owner. Can't call him up and ask him how it's doing.

But others have experimented with new wood building techniques. Mark Patty of Santa Rosa, California, built an epoxy-and-plywood Lightning 15 years ago.

I asked Mark how that boat compared to glass Lightnings.

Unlike WoodenBoat, whose Lightning was built with conventional frames along a backbone, Mark Patty chose to build his boat as if it were an airplane. He calls it the "stringer" method, and his very good how-to book is for sale by ILCA for $10.00

Anyway, instead of building frames and screwing, nailing or gluing planks or plywood over the frame, Mark built a skeleton resembling the frame of an airplane over which he placed sections of quarter-inch five-ply marine plywood. Because there is a compound curve on the bottom, plywood sections had to be fairly narrow – many pieces bend to shape easier than one or two big sections. Each piece of wood was coated with epoxy, and the plywood pieces also were glued with epoxy to the stringer frame. There are no metal fasteners in his boat.

For want of a better word, Mark calls the technique "cold-molding," though he admits the term is not quite apt because the Lightning has a hard chine. Cold-molded boats usually are soft chine boats, and the entire hull is made of plywood or other material glued together. Over the plywood, he glued pieces of 3/8-inch veneer to give the boat a rich, natural look. The veneer also adds to the overall strength of the boat.

So how did this woodie compare to fiberglass boats?

First, says Mark, "It was way stronger than even a plank boat. By the time you're done, it's all one piece. No seams, not a nail, no steel, no bronze, no staples, nothing left as far as hard fastenings."

> "From a maintenance standpoint, I don't think you're giving anything away to a fiberglass boat. In some ways, you're going to beat them, because the wood boat is not going to gain weight and the fiberglass core will suck up water."

Repair-wise, "You don't have loose screws and pop rivets to deal with."

"Fixing the wood boat is a heck of a lot easier than fixing a fiberglass boat. If somebody rakes off your rubrail, you smooth it out and paste on another piece. You get your plane out and plane the thing down and put another piece in and fair it all back together."

In terms of upkeep, "I was racing in salt water. When I finished, I'd rinse the boat off and hit the bar."

"From a maintenance standpoint, I don't think you're giving anything away to a fiberglass boat. In some ways, you're going to beat them, because the wood boat is not going to gain weight and the fiberglass core will suck up water. When my boat was built, we had 40 pounds of lead in it. Towards the end, I think I maybe took off 10 pounds of lead. It gained 10 pounds in 15 years. Not too many fiberglass boats are going to do as well as that."

He and his crew were rough on the deck, and every couple years he'd re-varnish it. "A new coat of varnish and it looked like new." Several years after he launched it, the deck began to show wear, so he painted it white. "What do you do with a fiberglass boat when it starts getting chalky? When a woody gets ratty, you paint it."

Where trailer bunks sometimes create soft spots in glass bottoms, Patty never had that problem.

Once in 15 years, he flipped the boat, sanded the bottom and re-varnished it with linear polyurethane.

What about speed? It was a competitive boat, but not as fast as his best glass boat. Why? Mark experimented with the shape of the bottom, hoping for a hull that would really scoot downwind.

"It wasn't as fast as my fiberglass boat, but it could have been if I hadn't screwed with it," he says.

When I was sailing 5885, I learned about wood on glass confrontations. As we slowly maneuvered onto our hoist, I made one of those little navigational errors which caused the bow of my woody to bump my neighbor's glass hull.

Bump?

My stem punched a hole that cost me $100 to have fixed.

Mark Patty noticed a reluctance of glass boat sailors to come close to his boat. It was a great advantage on the starting line and near marks. And it wasn't fear of being clobbered.

"They didn't want to hurt the pretty boat."

THE LINGO OF LIGHTNINGS

Plug Nickel is looking good!

The language of boating is a wonderful thing. When Patrick O'Brian describes studdingsails "aloft and alow," you visualize great clouds of canvas over a tiny bark. But the lingo of boating also can be obscure, especially to newcomers.

When my mother-in-law and her then 7-year-old daughter took up sailing years ago, they thought some of the basic commands seemed reasonable. "Ready about" was plenty clear. But others were a bit opaque. "Hard alee" seemed like a term easy to forget in the panic of a course change. They agreed on their own command for a tack.

We used to hear it piping across the waves of Georgian Bay, followed by peals of laughter.

"Ready about, . . . chandelier!"

I recalled the chandelier story late one night recently on a visit to Nickels Boat Works in Fenton. After months of talking about finishing Plug Nickel, Dave Nickels and I had agreed to meet at his shop and begin installing hardware on the finished hull.

I was trying to tell Dave that I wanted a simple boomvang on this boat, nothing elaborate. But it was late, and suddenly I could not remember that term, "boomvang." I suppose I could have said, "The thing that tightens the boom down in a following wind." Surely he'd never have figured out what I meant by "chandelier."

When I finally remembered the word and mentioned it, Dave pointed to his list. "Boomvang simple system." Already thought of.

David Nickels "translating" Joel's hardware requests.

For those who are just tuning in, nearly six years ago in a huge wave of enthusiasm for preserving and owning and sailing wooden boats, I bought the last wooden Lightning hull produced by the Nickels & Holman firm founded by Dave's father, Herman Nickels, in the late 1940s. This hull was built as a normal cedar-plank-on-mahogany frame Lightning sailboat. The deck is plywood covered with fiberglass with a textured rough, anti-slip pattern. The boat was never launched. It was used for years as a plug, or male mold, for making the female molds which were used to form fiberglass Lightnings. The boat Dave Nickels built in fall 1965 is the direct progenitor of all fiberglass Nickels & Holman Lightnings. In earlier issues of the Flashes, I've described the pitfalls I met in making it into a sailable craft.

Over the summers of 1998-99, Ron Sell, a professional boatbuilder who lives on a lake near Dexter, Michigan, had faired, fiberglassed and painted the hull. Last fall, I brought the hull back to Fenton for installation of hardware. Somehow, it had taken several months for us to concoct a plan of attack. Now we were rolling Plug Nickel out of the big Nickels Boat Works shed and into the finishing room. We dusted the deck and washed off the bird poop and lo and behold, it was a pretty boat again.

I was soon tripping over words. Five years ago, shortly after I bought the hull and hauled it home, I faxed a list to Dave of hard-

**What is this part of a sailboat called?
A. Console   B. Tray   C. Dashboard
D. Chandelier   E. All of the above**

ware I thought it needed. I was trying to imagine every piece of metal the boat might want. On the list was the word "console." Now, in June 2000, Dave was trying to figure out what that meant. Meanwhile, I was trying to parse his language. Because I work with radios, I use the word "console" for a device that contains electronic controls switches, meters, that sort of thing. It seemed natural to name the place on a boat where controls were found "console." Why not?

Dave kept referring to something called the "tray." The word sounded so unusual to me that I wasn't sure I'd heard it right. "Tray" this and "tray" that. Finally, he suggested that I crawl under an upside-down, new Lightning and have a look. I got down on my hands and knees and peered up. "You're looking at the wrong thing," he said.

Then he pointed to the console. It's a ledge or shelf running between the incomplete V-shape of the forward area of the cockpit. Right behind the mast, it's a perfect place for cam cleats that secure the various ropes that control jib and spinnaker. There, that's what I mean by "control."

Imagine, though, what Dave was thinking when he read on my list: "2 sets of blocks for mid-deck console controls."

Console is a word from motorboating, Dave points out. One guy he knows even calls the tray the "dashboard."

Why tray? "I don't know," says Dave. "I know that 'barber-hauler' is named after the Barber twins of California they were Lightning sailors in the sixties. I know 'cunningham' is named for Briggs Cunningham," a 1950s sailor.

Before I left my house in Plymouth, I loaded a full deck cover, a box full of bungie cords and a set of trailer lights in case a miracle happened and we installed the hardware. I figured if we installed the chainplates and the top gudgeon for the lightboard, I could trail it home and install the rest of the hardware. By the end of the evening, we had not drilled one hole and I realized that there was more to this hardware business than I realized.

Plug Nickel has a console, too. Or is it a tray?

For instance, the cables which attach through the deck by shackles to the jib commonly called the "cloth" and the "wire." Turns out these cables are fed under the deck via a pair of stainless steel tubes which are set into the wood with epoxy. Not something I would ever have imagined. Having built a lot of wooden Lightnings, Dave knows.

Or another useful fact: Dave quizzed me, "What are the floorboards for?"

"To keep you from stubbing your toes on the ribs," I said.

Floorboards are part of the structure, Dave said. It's not good to walk directly on the bottom of the boat, which after all consists of cedar planks attached to the frames by screws. The floorboards distribute your weight across several frames, preventing the load from falling directly on the hull planks.

Seats have a structural purpose, as well. Their horizontal braces attach to vertical braces on the centerboard trunk. Pressure from the seat frames helps prevent centerboard trunk warping.

At the end of the evening, I'd learned lots of useful things about Lightnings.

But I had a decision to make. Should I call it a console or a tray?

I had a second thought: I'll let my crew decide.

Chandelier.

BE SEATED, PLEASE

Let's talk today about some of the dilemmas a skipper faces when planning the rig of a new-old boat like Plug Nickel. But first, just let me quickly mention something that's been bothering me.

I'm wondering if maybe "Plug Nickel" is not the most apt name for my wooden Lightning.

How about ADD?

For "attention deficit disorder."

Take it from me, anyone who buys a sailboat hull and plans to equip it with mast, boom, sails, centerboard, rudder, hardware, hardware, hardware, had best reflect on what else he or she is getting with that stripped-clean hull: A passle of sidetracks. Diversions. Little sideshows that can, if you're not careful, overwhelm and dwarf the original project.

I've mentioned that I was lucky enough to possess such necessities as a stainless steel centerboard, and I bought not one, but two, yes, count them, oval Bryant masts. Second-hand, of course. I didn't have a boom, but why sweat the small stuff?

Through an ad in the Flashes, I was acquiring various hardware, almost new sails, a selection of rudders. I now have a new Nickels trailer for the boat and my choice of cockpit, trailing and full-hull mooring covers. There are rewards to being a scrounge.

One thing I didn't have was the sort of thing it's easy to set aside, mentally. Seats. I mean, who thinks about seats when you're busy trying to bludgeon an inch and a half of stubborn plastic off your hull because it was originally used to shape fiberglass molds?

But last year, when I delivered the finished, freshly painted hull to Nickels Boat Works in Fenton, it occurred to me that sailing this boat, even if it were fully equipped with the latest rigging and sails, would not be very comfortable without seats.

And seating was an amenity which this boat did not have.

Remember, it was the last woodie Nickels & Holman made

before they switched production to glass boats. They planned to use it as a plug, or male mold, for making female molds. They were not planning to mold the seats.

I remember last year pulling out my ILCA blueprints of the Lightning and finding no plans for seats. I called Dave Nickels for advice and learned that no plans remain for the Nickels & Holman wooden Lightning seats.

Now a real woodworker would not have seen this as a problem. Your real woodworker would simply have made some measurements and drawn up his or her own plans.

But I am a sometime woodworker, a guy who worked a few months in a woodshop as a belt sander many years ago. A guy who doesn't have the foggiest idea how to go about making plans for seats.

I tried to imagine sailing Plug Nickel without seats. I couldn't imagine my wife getting aboard, let alone taking a seat not to be had.

Above: The long part of the seat. At stern in middle are two pieces which were then unrouted. These are the pieces I mistakenly cut with the grain at right angles to the keel. Wrong. Weak. Could break. Do it over right. Below: Shows seats at stern, including the mis-cut center pieces not yet routed or sanded.

Then I saw the ad in Flashes. It was placed by Craig Kvalle of Cleveland. I remembered Craig. He'd offered to sell me his race-rigged Nickels & Holman # 6279 a couple years back and in a moment of clear-headed sanity I'd declined. What would I do with a second wooden Lightning when I was overloaded trying to restore the first one? Craig had sent me photos showing a pretty dark green boat on a trailer with a natural transom, oval mast and boom, but I didn't bite.

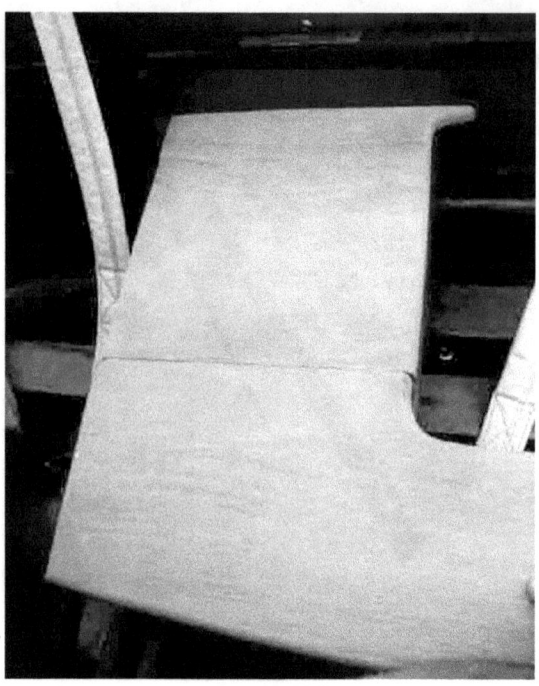

The forward part of the seat. Wood is 3/4 inch thick Honduran mahogany (should have been 5/8, but hated to destroy the wood). Note the ear which fits fine on this boat, #6279. The ear must be removed for use in Plug Nickel.

Something about the ad last fall triggered my mad desire to own this boat. I made the call, found that Craig was in a hurry to get rid of it. For $500, he would deliver it to my warehouse in Plymouth. There were little extras: The original wooden boom, though the wooden mast was long gone. Sails for the original wooden rig as well as fairly fresh modern sails. A nice cover which it turned out would need $70 in repairs. And a pretty decent trailer.

Now here is what clinched it. This boat, I reasoned, is a Nickels & Holman with the same seats as my plug. Forget drawing plans. Just pull the seats from this boat and use them as patterns.

Problem solved!

Carried forward by the power of my own impeccable logic, I agreed to buy this old woodie.

Now, you see what I mean about diversions? No?

Well consider – it's one more boat that needs to be licensed. Needs to be cared for in terms of protecting it from rain. The very nice cover turned out to have a weak spot which I felt obliged to have repaired. And running my eyes over the rig, I can't help but feel this boat deserves to have a traditional wood or at least square aluminum track mast instead of the modern oval aluminum spar. As I identify with the latest boat, new projects appear. Time and money are diverted from Plug Nickel.

But you can't deny that one thing this boat has is the original seats.

What it didn't have was a name. At first, I was calling it the "Five Hundred," in an effort to emphasize to me and my wife how cheap it was. I have to admit that it was some weeks after I bought this boat that I finally admitted to Karen what I'd done.

I've decided, finally, to use her name: "Dumb Ass Idea."

With Plug Nickel waiting in Fenton to have hardware installed, by late fall there wasn't much I could do on the project. So I carefully unscrewed the seats from Dumb Ass Idea, measured the pieces and drove to Milford, MI where I bought some beautiful Honduran mahogany from a dealer called Armstrong Millworks. Now I needed a way to cut the mahogany. At Armstrong, they recommended a used tool dealer in Holly, MI.

This is where the really serious ADD comes in. Impelled by the feeling that I needed a tool to properly cut the expensive mahogany I'd just bought, I visited the tool dealer and wound up buying a Delta 14-inch industrial bandsaw. At the dealer's urging, I decided to spend some time last winter dismantling the saw, stripping layers of paint and re-painting it industrial gray. While I still believe it's a far finer tool than I could buy from a new equipment dealer, the day-long restoration project the dealer outlined for me turned out to be a gross underestimate. Now re-painted, the saw is ready to be re-assembled, but it was not ready when I wanted to cut my mahogany for the seats last spring. To tell you the truth, it still is not assembled six months later.

So guess what: I pulled out my trusty saber saw, which I had all along, and did the job as I could have done it last fall without buying a bandsaw.

Do I regret the bandsaw? No. It's a fine tool that will cut either metal or wood and one I could not have afforded to buy new.

As to the seats, that project was very satisfying. I got great pleasure from rough cutting the seats with my saber saw. Then I used the original seats as a guide and with a straight router bit I fine cut the new wood with the router by using the cutter bearing to follow the old seat while the blade formed the shape of the new seat. I used the router again to make a curve on the top and bottom edges of the seats where legs won't like sharp edges.

Last fall, I tried the original seats in Plug Nickel, and they worked fine with one exception. The forward parts of the seats where they cross the cockpit and butt against the centerboard trunk have ears or tails on the old boat. On my newer boat, a pair of vertical seat braces leaves no room for the tails. I forgot that detail because there was a months-long delay between the original fitting last fall and my cutting efforts in May. So, while my new seats fit perfectly in the old boat, they are not quire correct for the Plug. Minor corrections will be needed.

More serious, I discovered that I have cut two small stern pieces so the grain would run perpendicular to the keel. Dave Nickels warned me these pieces are inherently weak and could break.

So I have to re-cut those small pieces, and guess what: I don't have quite enough wood for the very last piece.

What to do?

No, I'm not making another trip to Armstrong Millworks.

That would be a sidetrack.

I'll just glue and clamp two pieces of mahogany and be done with it.

Enough about seats. Who cares about seats, anyway?

Let's see, we were going to talk about rigging . . .

TAPE RULE

Having confessed in a previous column to my latest indiscretion involving a wooden Lightning, I find myself breathing freer. There is a spring in my step. I feel like a man who has rid himself of a tremendous burden of guilt.

For all those months I carried alone the burden of knowing I'd committed that worst of sins – I bought yet another wooden sailboat.

Now some related news from the Thurtell Boatworks.

Last week, I proudly showed longtime Lightning sailor and wooden boat restorer John Young my now guilt-free second wooden Nickels & Holman, #6279, aka Dumb Ass Idea. John admired the interior brightwork, and then began to inspect the fiberglass on the bottom. Hmmm, he said. That doesn't look good.

Sure enough, what I had failed to notice in some eight months of ownership, John picked out almost instantly. Or maybe this is a recent development. I was aware that a previous owner had installed a fiberglass sheath on the boat's bottom. What I had not noticed was this three-foot crack all the way through the glass, running from near the chine to the keelson. Whoops. When did that appear? I had plans of putting this boat in the water. Not so fast. To launch the boat in this condition would be foolish. Water would flow between the glass and wood hull and might start the process of rot.

Start it?

> **I was aware that a previous owner had installed a fiberglass sheath on the boat's bottom. What I had not noticed was this three-foot crack all the way through the glass, running from near the chine to the keelson. Whoops. When did that appear?**

Lightning 6279. Some consider it not a good idea.

Hah!

Lucky if it isn't already well on its way.

We discussed solutions. All seemed to call for turning the boat over, removing the glass and either replacing some planks or replacing the bottom.

How easy it is for one man to tell another all the steps he needs to take to fix a boat.

Let's step back for a moment. Recall that I'm the guy who already has a wooden boat named Plug Nickel which I bought in 1994. I figured I'd be sailing it in summer 1995. Well, the boat may or may not touch water in the year of our lord 2000, six years after the project began. One of the major brakes on that project was more than 100 pounds of hard resin I had to remove from the bottom.

So any thought of replacing the bottom on yet another boat starts to make me seasick. Plug Nickel must come first, anyway. I may suffer from attention deficit disorder, but I do have some control.

As I see it, I have one of two choices:

1) I can flip the boat over and spend the next six years tinkering with the bottom, all the time fantasizing what it will be like to sail 6279 when it's finished.

2) I can seal the crack quickly but temporarily and sail Dumb Ass Idea now.

What would you do?

Well, I do have what passes for a plan.

Hint: I'm in something of a hurry, on account of my incredible good luck, thanks to a Flashes classified ad, in locating and buying a good wooden Lightning mast and boom.

Last year, Dumb Ass Idea arrived at my warehouse with an oval aluminum mast and boom. At the time, the modern touches seemed the big selling point. My original plan was to sail it with the modern rig. Know what? That sounds boring. Now that I'm ready to sail 6279, or DAI, it appears that I'll have a nice old wooden mast to put on it.

And that sounds like fun. Exciting enough fun to make me want to get aboard this "new" 1956 boat.

Now, not in 2006.

So how to seal that crack?

I murmured my solution and got a word of caution from my 17-year-old son:

"Don't use duct tape, Dad."

Why not?

Because, Abe says, Popular Science tested various tapes and found that duct tape is the worst tape there is. Even as duct tape, it's the worst.

Well, if not duct tape, what?

The whole point of this column was to brag about fixing a boat with tape.

So I'm locked into tape. I know –- I'll try that fiberglass reinforced packing tape.

Hey, we're not going to circumnavigate the world.

There you have it, folks –- yet another high-tech tip on wooden boat restoration, thanks to your Cedar & Spruce columnist.

We're on the cutting edge here –- this is a big experiment.

Tell you how it works later.

Gotta tape that boat.

FEAR OF DRILLING

So there I was cruising the Interstate, happy thoughts in my head with tree limbs swaying in the wind. We were going sailing, there was breeze, and all was right with the world. Even better, I'd made great progress that morning on my current obsession, the rigging of my wooden Lightning known as Plug Nickel.

Besides chainplates, Plug Nickel now has barber-hauler blocks and spinnaker sheet cam cleats.

I admit it. I was gloating a bit, patting myself on the back for the wonderful craftsmanship I'd imposed on the stern of that woodie as I sweated under the morning sun drilling holes, slapping hardware and cranking screws.

A picture floated into my mind's eye – a picture of the changes I'd made in the boat. Then another picture intruded – a picture of the stern of another boat I'd studied earlier in our boat club parking lot.

Suddenly, I was yelling.

"I screwed up! Oh, no! I blew it!"

From the seat next to me, my wife looked at me curiously. In the back seat, my 17-year-old son said nothing.

They're used to this.

My worst nightmare had happened.

This was the day when I'd taken my own

Chainplate – the first cuts in the virgin deck were by Dave Nickels.

independent steps towards finishing Plug Nickel. Finally, I had overcome the phobia which for roughly a year stopped me from rigging my beloved wooden Lightning that was built 35 years ago and never launched. Last fall, I'd delivered the boat to its original builder, Dave Nickels of Nickels Boat Works in Fenton, Mich. Newly refinished inside and out, the boat was back in Fenton for Dave to install hardware and make it ready to sail. We were going to work on it together, but after our schedules conflicted a couple times I decided to do it myself. In August, nearly a year later, I hauled the boat back to my place.

Rudder sitting in newly-installed gudgeons – More holes drilled, and the rudder works great in the parking lot.

Putting hardware on a sailboat can't be that big a deal, I told myself.

As he helped tighten the trailer straps, Dave's brother, George Nickels, opined that, "Rigging a Lightning is a complicated job."

Maybe so, I thought, but I can do it!

Still, I had a problem: I had this boat that was real pretty, but its deck was just so pristine. What if I measured wrong or misunderstood or somehow basically screwed up – as I am wont to do – and wound up disfiguring or even wrecking the boat?

It helped earlier in the summer to watch Dave cut the slots for the chainplates. He'd simply drilled overlapping holes until he had four neat slots in the deck, two on either side. Those were the first cuts in that deck, and the moment seemed matter of fact, not at all climactic. At home, I installed the chainplates through those slots. But that didn't call for making new holes in the deck. All I had to do was make sure my stainless steel screws were 5/8-inch long – or rather, 5/8 inch short, so they would not pierce the hull from the inside out.

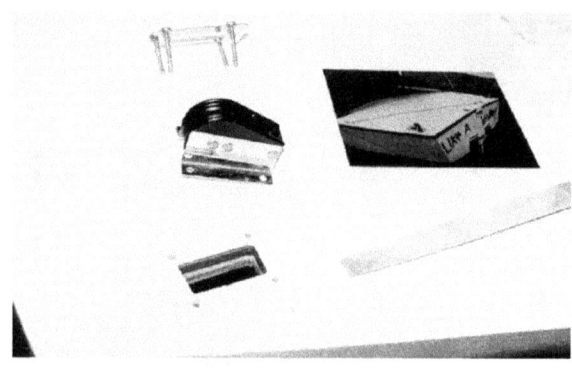

Spinnaker block ready for mounting. Note photo of another boat showing placement.

And oh, by the way, don't let that drill bit go all the way through, either!

I carefully measured and measured again to mount my gudgeons, and those were now nice and level and centered correctly. I knew they were right because I'd mounted my trusty kick-up rudder in them and it swung back and forth just fine.

Perhaps my gudgeon success made me overconfident.

Maybe I just got overwhelmed by the big picture and failed to tend to details. Conceptual details.

"Rigging a Lightning is a complicated job."

Oh, yes.

Just installing the backstay is complicated. Here's how it works. The steel backstay cable from the mast attaches by shackle to a block which runs along a nylon cord. The cord makes an inverted V over the transom of the boat. One end of the cord passes through a fairlead under the deck and attaches to the inside by a gudgeon bolt. The other leg of the V passes through the deck via a deck-mounted turning block and goes forward about a foot or so where it is tied by bowline to a double turning block. Three cheek blocks mounted under the forward end of the stern deck direct the backstay control rope back to and through the double block. The control rope makes that trip twice. The outer two cheek blocks point each end of the control rope to starboard and port turning blocks which make roughly right angles, passing the control rope to additional blocks which angle the rope to cam cleats on either side of the deck about midway along the cockpit.

Got it?

Why, it sounded so simple that when the plan blew away, I

didn't get upset.

Later that day, as we drove along the freeway, I reviewed what I'd done that morning. That memory of another Lightning with what had to be the correct mounting of the backstay block juxtaposed with my mind's picture of how I'd done it.

The two pictures did not agree.

The blocks I installed were off by 90 degrees.

Whoops.

Why I mounted the backstay turning block pointed port and starboard instead of fore and aft, I can't explain.

Maybe I was so preoccupied with the big picture that I lost my grasp of the details.

But, oh, man!

Despite my fears, my extra care, I'd done it. Messed up my boat.

Why, in the first place, was I so afraid to do it?

Fear of making a mistake.

Fear of drilling: Here was a classic boat, built according to traditional wooden boat techniques by a pro, Dave Nickels of what was then Nickels & Holman. In the mid-1960s, N & H was a leading manufacturer of Lightning sailboats. Now the boat – used by its original maker as a mold for making glass Lightnings – belongs to me. It is my responsibility to restore it without somehow crippling it.

And who am I to do this job?

The wrong guy, maybe. Not a trained boat builder. Just a writer, a guy who lives a lot of his life in his mind, nurturing fantasies about boats. Oh yes, I worked in a wood shop briefly as a belt sander, so I know a very little bit about power tools. Very little. I spend most of my days on the phone or pounding a keyboard for my job as a newspaper reporter.

That drill gaffe occurred on Saturday morning of Labor Day weekend. I had planned to make lots of progress with the hardware in those three days. Instead, I spent a good deal of Sunday fixing my error. In fact, I was still fixing it the following weekend.

Fortunately, I had not yet cut the rectangular hole to seat the block. I am left with three small holes which serve no purpose.

What to do? I will fill them. I will paint the filler white like the rest of the deck. I will do my best to hide them.

If only I could stop myself moaning about it!

Slowly, I am adjusting to my mistake.

First, I've come to understand it was not so bad. Three wrong holes, no big deal.

Groan!

Second, I am coaching myself to go even slower, think things through again and again. Remember, I tell myself, you are not a boatbuilder. You are a writer. You have to take extra care.

Slowly, with lots of reflection, I'm finishing the backstay installation, pondering if it will interact (hopefully not) with the boom bridle which I've now decided to put in.

I'm giving lots of thought to the forestay fitting, because that oddity really calls for some fancy drilling right through the deck and into the stem.

While it makes me nervous, I'm excited about doing the work.

Despite my goofs, I'm enjoying this business of putting hardware on my Lightning.

It is worth getting scared and excited about.

When I'm done, I will have rigged a Lightning.

And that is a complicated job.

ANATOMY OF A SCREW-UP

"I put on my first coat of varnish on the interior wood, BUT it's not drying. Perhaps the sealer I used is either incompatible or did not dry completely before I put the varnish over it. BIG MESS. I'm asking around for help on this problem now."

That e-mail came to me a few days ago from Posey Hedges, a Lightning sailor from Memphis, TN who is restoring a 1950s kitbuilt Lightning. (Follow Posey's adventures on-line at www.memphissoundworks.com/ lightning.html)

Amateur that I am at boat restoration, I could not offer Posey any advice on how to salvage the dripping mess of varnish. But I can guess how this screw-up came about. In the last few years of hassling with my own Lightning restoration, I have learned lots about how disasters come about.

In my last column, I howled and groaned so long about various mistakes I'd made, mainly with my beloved cordless drill, that I decided to step back and try to figure out why I was messing up.

Then I received the e-mail from Posey, who until that point in our electronic correspondence had seemed to be coolly in control of his own woodie project. As I considered how it might come about that varnish would not dry, I reflected on my most recent botch-ups.

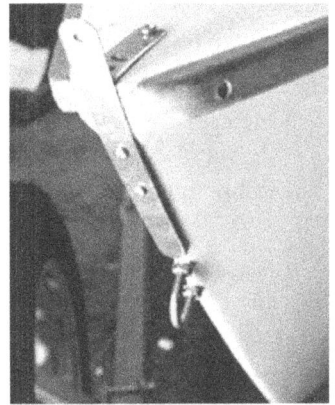

Suddenly one day, Plug Nickel was sporting this shiny forestay fitting. That's when it truly became a sailboat. A sailboat needs a mast, and a mast needs to be attached to the hull. Chainplates went on for the port and starboard shrouds, followed by the backstay and now the forestay.

I had only to recall as far back as last weekend, when I lay on my belly in the bow of Plug Nickel, mahogany frames poking my ribs and the sweet stink of epoxy filling my nose. Shining into the top corner of the bow was a flashlight, wedged against the V of the first frame. The beam illuminated my right hand, holding a plastic food container with a syrupy concoction of WEST System epoxy thickened to what I hoped was a peanut butter consistency. With my left hand, I was lifting sticky dabs of epoxy and pushing them into a yawning hole in the stem. As much as I pushed the glue into the hole, it ran right back out and seemed unwilling to harden the way epoxy is supposed to. Meanwhile, epoxy was dribbling down the stem and clogging the threads of the twin bow eye bolts which needed to stay clear so they could take nuts and serve as an anchor point for my centerboard block-and-tackle hoist system.

As I lay there inhaling all sorts of wonderful fumes, including the acetone I used to clean those bolt threads, it occurred to me that screw-ups occur because of failures in one or more of the following areas:

Concept
Training
Work area
Organization
Time

Concept

What I mean by concept is simply having a general idea of how the job is supposed to look when it's finished. Here's a recent example -- from today, as a matter of fact. A box arrived yesterday from Nickels Boat Works and inside was a stainless steel cylinder surrounding a bolt with a cam cleat at its head. The cylinder is attached to a bracket. This is the device which secures the end of the rope that does the heavy lifting for a centerboard block-and-tackle hoist. I'd seen this before on other people's boats, but never gave it a thought. But now I'm trying to make it work on my 1965 woodie, and I have a big question. Is that swivel supposed to turn 360 degrees? Because if so, it won't work on my boat. Unlike today's glass boats, my wooden Nickels &

Holman has a beautiful mahogany centerboard trunk capped with a flat piece of mahogany which extends about an inch and a half to either side of the actual trunk. If my swivel is bracketed to that trunk, it will hit that cap. Of course, if it doesn't have to turn 360 degrees, there's no worry.

A quick call to Dave Nickels confirms, however, that it should spin all the way around.

Now that I'm clear on the idea, the solution is simple: Screw a piece of wood to the centerboard trunk so that the swivel is bracketed away from the trunk cap. That's easier said than done, though, simply because I can't just slap any old board on this boat. A beautiful mahogany CB trunk deserves a piece of mahogany and it should be varnished to a sheen equal to the trunk itself. This is how not days, but weeks are added to each piece of this project. Now there's a trip to a specialty lumber yard, followed by measuring, sawing, sanding and varnishing. I thought I'd have that hoist working today, but what's another couple weeks in a project that's already six years old?

With the addition of the forestay hardware, Plug Nickel finally qualifies as a sailboat. It has all the proper points for attaching a mast.

Concept – it means knowing which way a lead block points before you drill holes the wrong way. It means foreseeing how an oddly-shaped forestay fitting will mount INSIDE your stem, and just how much wood and in what angular direction to gouge out so that fitting will work – without removing so much wood that you have to lie in the bow pasting epoxy into the cavern you made because your idea of the lay of the forestay was in error.

Training

All I mean by training, really, is experience enough that you don't make beginner's errors when you're trying to accomplish a task which deserves journeyman effort. Unfortunately for weekend boat restorers like me, most tasks come with no introduction. This is no kit, with step-by-step plans and how-to explanations. It's do-it-yourself, from stem to stern, believe me.

In the example above, I could have saved myself a lot of trouble and eliminated much of my mess had I known that the epoxy would take more than half an hour to begin setting up. When it finally began to harden, I could feel it -- the plastic holder got too hot to handle. Chalk that one up. Next time, I'll mix my epoxy, set it down, do something else with a timer set so I periodically feel the container. When it starts to get warm, I know it's time to begin cramming putty-like plastic wherever it needs to go.

But there's more to the story. For instance, why was I plastering plastic into a hole way up in the bow of my boat? Because I went a little too far with my drill one sunny day. Why did that happen? Because I had a very fuzzy idea of how a certain forestay fitting should be attached to my boat.

Work area

Hemingway said it: "A Clean, Well-Lighted Place."

When the weather was still warm, I did my boat work outdoors because it seemed easier than the enormous job of organizing my ham radio warehouse to make room for about 23 feet of boat and trailer. Making things harder is the fact that the only way I can get a boat into this place is through my machinist neighbor's paint shop, which has a sliding door leading to my workshop. When my neighbor's paint shop is busy, he can't accommodate my need to move a boat through his area. So I have to time my move to periods when his shop is relatively empty. For those reasons, I preferred to work outside.

But that meant not working when it was dark or raining. As cold weather threatened, I finally admitted the obvious -- that a day of labor devoted to carving a hole in my shop would multiply the time I would have to work on the boat by letting me have those dark or rainy hours.

Organization and time

I find that my ability to organize a particular task is directly linked to the amount of time I have available. Often, it turns out that I've under-estimated how much time a task will need. No, correction, ALWAYS, I find I've under under-rated time needs. Unconsciously, the need to move quickly is always present, and it stresses my mental processes. I may have carefully thought out step-by-step procedures, but under pressure to move things along, I often forget important steps. Or I may mentally set aside the inter-relationship of today's project with something that must follow, or even something that already has been done.

Having enough time is just as important as having a good place to work, in my estimation.

I came home last Saturday a bit hang-dog because my epoxy job in the boat's nose had not gone according to plan. "What's the big hurry?" asked my wife. Good question. There should be no hurry. What was my rush? I have to admit that in my mind's eye I saw myself playing with that neat centerboard hoist system, showing it off. I was too eager to make the fantasy real.

Then today while jogging I recalled a solution I conceived a long time ago for filling that gaping hole with epoxy. I was going to cut a piece of wood such that it would cover the hole. It would be tacked across the rear top of the stem, just under the deck There would be a hole in the top of the little board. I even bought a medicine syringe, the kind you use to give a kid liquid medications. I would use the syringe to pump epoxy into the cavity. The board would hold the epoxy in place. No mess.

What happened to that idea? Time crunch. It got lost in the labyrinth of my imagination as I rushed to finish the job.

Eventually, this whole Plug Nickel dream will be real and I'll be sailing this light blue boat on Cass Lake or Georgian Bay and then what?

I'll miss all the how-do-I-do-it fantasies, the minute mental planning, drawing rigging layouts on scraps of paper, multiple trips to hardware and boat supply stores and the fun of making it all work right.

And yes, I'll probably miss that other thing that I hate so much

> **Despite all the angst of the last few months, there have been moments of triumph. One of those occurred when I demonstrated to family and friends how the backstay ropes glide back and forth through all their blocks, making it possible for me to adjust mast tension from either side of the boat. What a fantastic sound, ropes running through blocks!**

right now – the anguish of the screw-up.

Despite all the angst of the last few months, there have been moments of triumph. One of those occurred when I demonstrated to family and friends how the backstay ropes glide back and forth through all their blocks, making it possible for me to adjust mast tension from either side of the boat. What a fantastic sound, ropes running through blocks!

A bigger victory appeared when I stood back and admired that forestay fitting as it sat firmly screwed onto the stem of my boat. The moment seemed like a watershed. First the chainplates went on. Then the backstay. Now, with the forestay fitting, I could ship a mast any time.

This was no longer a plug. It is now a boat.

SIDE SHOW

How could you bear to cut holes in the deck of your boat? For once, someone else was wailing about something I'd done to Plug Nickel. I'd e-mailed Flashes Editor Karen Johnson the latest images of my work on the sailboat of my dreams.

One was a shot of Plug Nickel right after I sawed a 3 1/2-by-11-inch hole on the starboard side of the deck, midway along the cockpit.

What was I, nuts?

I'd made a picture window into the bottom of my boat.

A gaping hole the leaping waves were bound to find.

No sooner had I cut that hole than I walked around the boat with my trusty drill and made the holes to start sawing the mirror image of that hole on the port side.

These destructive shenanigans took place the weekend of December 2-3, year 2000. I recall being in a euphoric mood most of that Saturday and Sunday. For once, things were going my way.

I was following my own rules now. I'd allowed myself plenty of time for this job of radical surgery. My boat was in my shop with plenty of light and heat and a roof to keep tons of snow off my work.

Still, this was a difficult move to make, mentally. Cutting gaping holes in my boat seemed wrong. Karen was correct – how could I contemplate such an act?

It was fully premeditated. I'd gone over every step in my head. My digital camera was lying nearby to record every step of the procedure.

And no, I was not nuts.

I was improving my old wooden Lightning.

Modernizing it.

The idea came from Dave Nickels of Nickels Boat Works.

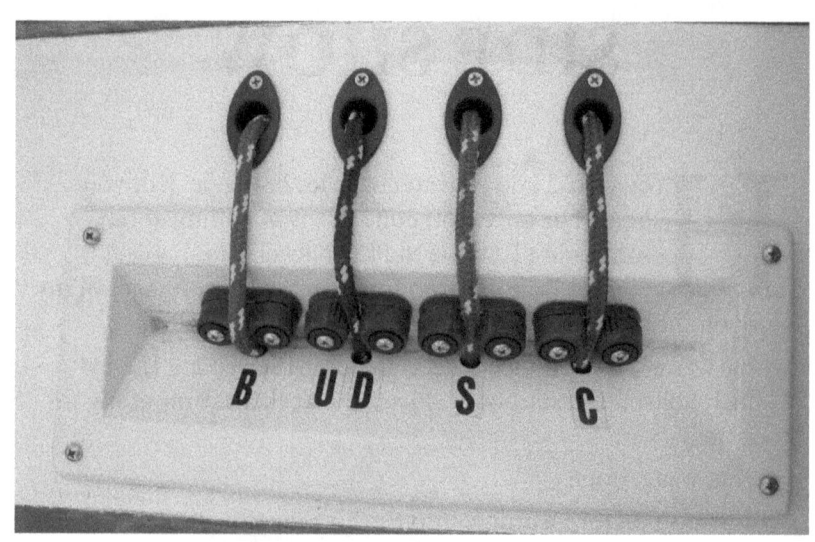

Side control panel on port side, looking outward. Controls are 1) Backstay; 2) Bridle, up-down; 3) Bridle, sideways; 4) Cunningham

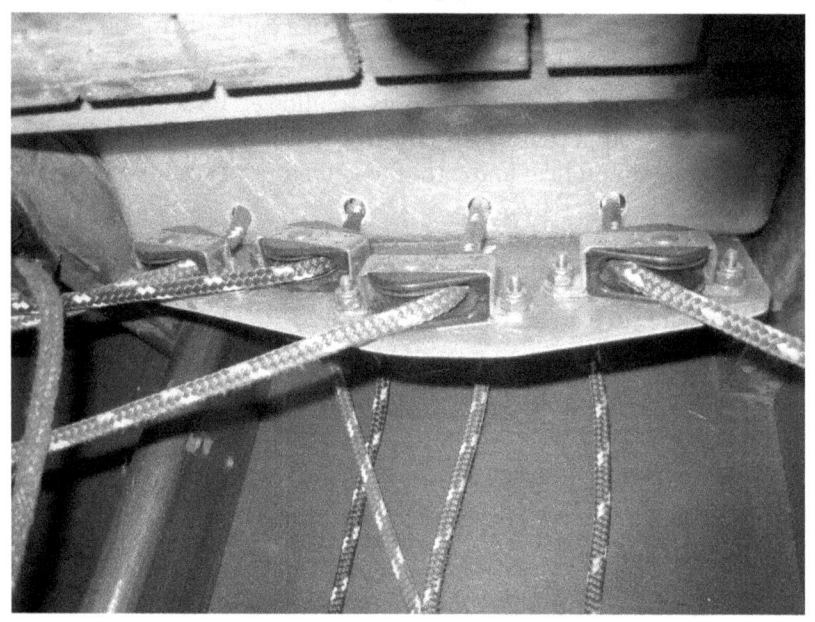

View of side panel, port side, under deck

It was quite a departure from the way I thought about this project last summer, when I'd been talking simplicity, simplicity. Now, you could say that was a natural attitude, given that my boat was built in 1965, when Lightning rigging was less complex than it is now. So a simple rig would be more in keeping with the – whoops, I was about to say antique character of my boat. Except that throughout this project, I've always had a conflicting set of goals. Why not consider the plug a clean slate and rig it as if it were a newly made boat? That is a leitmotif I've adopted and rejected many times.

One school of thought says that to be historically accurate, I ought to rig this boat with the hardware that was current in 1965, when Dave Nickels built it. I've pretty much rejected that idea. I plan to sail this boat for a long time. Any my wife and sons will be sailing it, too. We've sailed plenty in old boats, and I know that I don't want any more winches in my boat. I'll use a block and tackle to raise my centerboard. Same with my jib uphaul. I may be wedded to wood, but I'm the first to admit there are some new approaches to rigging Lightnings that make life a lot easier for sailors.

However, there was another consideration. Namely, my own doubts about my ability to install the hardware that would support a modern rig. Early last summer, when I first began work on the hardware, I was all for simplicity because it looked like a way to get the metal on the boat quickly and easily. Honestly, had I known how complex the rigging would turn out to be, I probably would have stuck to simple.

But as I began installing individual pieces of stainless steel, I found myself enjoying the task. And the more hardware I installed, the more I looked and measured and looked again and studied both my boat and the pieces of steel which I intended to screw or bolt and sometimes even glue in place, the more confident I became.

So that when Dave Nickels came up with his idea for side controls last fall, I was all for it.

Turns out it's the first time anyone has put these side controls in a woodie, though it has been done on older glass boats.

Here's how it works. First, you have the backstay, which on a Lightning is capable of having its tension adjusted. The easy way to do that is by means of a rope leading out from under the stern deck to a cam cleat on the stern deck coaming. Originally, this was what I planned to do. But as I reflected on what it would be like to sail with that kind of backstay control, I hesitated. What if I were sitting forward and couldn't reach far back to the rear of the cockpit? Wouldn't it be more convenient to have that backstay control handy at the side of the deck? Indeed, it would be even better if it were on both sides of the deck.

Secondly, if I wanted to have a bridle for tightening the boom on close-hauled tacks, I'd need to make some holes in either side of the deck for those ropes. Two lines per side.

And then, what about the cunningham? Where was I going to run that control line?

I needed some way to bring four control lines per side – eight total – through the deck.

On the phone, I was quizzing Dave about this problem. I already had installed a backstay system with two cords running under port and starboard decks to cheek blocks, with cleats under the deck on both sides about even with the main cam cleat. Dual controls. But what about the bridle? That needed two lines. And the cunningham.

The solution?

"A side panel from a Rebel," Dave said.

What's this?

Nickels Boat Works makes Rebel sailboats. Early in production, before they were certain where the side controls would go, they made a separate two-part fiberglass housing which could be drilled to take four cam cleats and four cheek blocks. The cam cleats are mounted in a slanting depression in the deck panel. The blocks are mounted on a plate which attaches to the deck panel via the same bolts that secure the cam cleats.

On each panel, the three sternmost cam cleats have cheek blocks aimed backward for the two bridle controls and the backstay rope. The fourth, forward cam cleat has a cheek block aimed forward for the cunningham.

But here is the neat, serendipitous thing: There are 11 inches of space between the frames of a Lightning. And it turns out that the Rebel side panel will just fit into that space.

By cutting a 3 1/2-inch by 11-inch slot through my plywood deck, between two frames, I could slide this panel into the hole. Because the two frames were close and underneath the edges of the side control panel, I could drill four holes and screw the panel to the deck and into the frames. Very solid, very neat.

And that is what I did, after measuring and re-measuring, taking it slow and easy, re-thinking again. Finally, I drew lines for my slot, drilled a hole into the inner area to be cut out, grabbed my saber saw and began cutting. I had to be careful near the frames so that I didn't cut too far and injure a frame.

It worked amazingly well. However, the glass panel was a tad large. I filed the plywood deck and the frames until the panel would slide through easily. The final step will be to seal the space between the panel and deck with silicon grouting material.

This is a fairly easy way to modernize an old wooden or fiberglass boat.

Pleased with my handiwork, I wrote those words. The following weekend I laid grout on the underside of a panel, turned it over and screwed it into the starboard deck. I was short on time –- had to meet my son at the airport, so I decided to postpone putting in the final panel.

A week later, I found time to go over to my shop. I had it in mind to measure and cut holes for the barberhauler through-deck blocks. But first, I thought, I ought to install that last side control. So I set the panel upside down on a workbench and drew a bead of grout around the edge. Before setting it in place, I held it up and mentally ran the lines through the four cam cleats.

Something was wrong.

They didn't go.

I was trying to set this on the portside deck, but it was configured with cam cleats for the starboard side. This could not be!

In a panic, I ran around the boat and checked the starboard control panel. The backstay cord was in place, no problem. And the cam cleat next to it was fine.

It turns out that way back when, as I bolted the cam cleats into place, I made a mistake in placing the first two cleats on that panel. That caused me to delude myself into putting the panel on the wrong side.

And now it was glued in place.

I mean, it was hard as granite.

Or so it seemed.

One thing about that silicon grout material. It takes forever to harden, especially in a cold shop.

Despair was the name of my mental state. I forgot about those barberhauler deck blocks. Carefully, I tried slipping a putty knife under the fiberglass side control panel.

Yes!

I hurried out to the hardware store and bought several broad putty knives. Tapping the knives gently with a hammer, I managed to insert the flat blades under the fiberglass panel and slice through every square inch of grout. Slowly, I worked the panel up.

Whew!

Another screw-up corrected.

The cause? Partly, I was in a hurry to meet a plane the previous weekend.

But the prime cause of that mistake was simply not being attentive to how I was mounting the cam cleats and failing to double-check my work. I did that task a long time ago, moved on to other projects and didn't think to check.

By now, I've corrected all those mistakes. The side controls are in their proper places with cam cleats aimed the right way.

Even the barberhauler system is in place.

But I am moving much, much slower, measuring, thinking and re-thinking before I make any more radical cuts.

It's hard learning from my mistakes.

As I looked at that panel, with eight putty knives sticking out from under it, I thought of shooting a photo for the inevitable column.

Then I had a second thought: That is exactly the kind of distraction that got me into this jam!

Just do it – right!

MY FIRST BOAT

In January 1999, I began struggling against the idea of writing a wooden boat column for the Flashes. Recently, while perusing old files in my Mac, I discovered a piece dated two years ago with the title, Cedar and Spruce. It would be many more months before I submitted my first column to the Flashes, and when I wrote those columns, I had forgotten my first attempts. It occurred to me that the thoughts in that old file, which contains a rough outline for future columns and an essay about My First Boat, might be of some interest to Flashes readers. Here it is:

A month ago, the idea of writing a Flashes column about wooden Lightnings sounded as easy as sailing in light air. I'm a writer, I sail Lightnings and I fix up wooden boats. When Flashes editor Karen Johnson asked me, Would you write Cedar & Spruce, I said, Hey, easy. I can whip off two or three this afternoon!

Right away, I had doubts. What do I know about wooden boats, really? Have I ever worked in a wooden boat yard? No. Have I taken a class in wooden boat building or repair? No. Well, then, what are my qualifications?

Hmmm. I can write.

Big deal. So can lots of other people.

I was a belt sander in a wood shop once upon a time.

I have restored two wooden sailboats. Yes, I returned two old wrecks to sailing condition.

And I'm engaged in a third restoration project. Well, in fact even a fourth.

There's my 1965 Nickels & Holman plug project, and our 1947 Chris-Craft Deluxe Runabout.

Neither is an active project right now.

I hate to talk about my restoration projects. They are taking way too long to finish. It was that thought that brought on a bad case of writer's block. If I can't do my own boat restorations, what do I have to write about?

But it occurred to me that my lack of professional boat building credentials gives me some authority, after all. I have restored two boats despite my lack of professional experience. If I can do it, so can anyone.

I sure do know about the things that stop a person from fixing up a boat. Or at least slow the project down. Way down. Fact is, I have not worked on either of my wooden boats in months. Why?

The answer could inspire a column. But I could boil it down to one word.

Space.

Or lack of it.

Yes, having time or making time to work on the boat is important.

And yes, having money to start, let alone finish, the project is also important.

But I consider the space problem first because at the moment I have no place to work on my boats.

But even before space, time and money, there is a prerequisite. A fundamental condition which must be met.

Will.

Motivation.

What makes a person to want to build or restore a wooden boat?

A sailor friend, Wylie Gerdes, once listened to my long-winded narration of all the work I put into fixing up a 1953 Wagemaker Snipe. Having put the Snipe in the water, I launched into a description of my then current project – another 1953 Snipe. When I had brought that project up to date, Wylie remarked, "Either you work on boats, or you sail."

I hear his words again and again as I mess with my wooden boat projects.

Is there a way to do both, have your restoration project and also do some sailing?

I have tried it. For a long time, it didn't work. Why? Well, there is the question of just how many boats can you own? If your only boat is your restoration project, you're not going to do much sailing. That's how it was for me in the beginning. My first restoration project, that Wagemaker Snipe, was the only boat I had ever owned. So until I made it seaworthy, all of my sailing would be in my head.

Now, here is the story of that Snipe, my first b—

Whoops! I just remembered. The Snipe was not my first boat, after all. Yes, I see it now. It's not made of wood. It sure is ugly. And it doesn't run by sail.

But here it is. The story of . . .

My First Boat

In those days, the mid 1970s, we were living on a fruit farm about five miles west of Paw Paw, Michigan. An orchard of Jonathan trees nestled next to the old two-story farmhouse where we lived. Across the orchard and through a deep woods there was an 18-acre lake. Half of the shoreline was owned by our friends who owned the farm. The other half was owned by a neighboring fruit farmer.

Popendick Lake was known for its big small mouth bass, but the best way to catch them was to fish from a boat. There was no good shoreline for fishing. Popendick was a natural lake bounded by the Carlson and Hood farms, with no public access. You got to the shore by walking down a tractor lane that ended at the lake. Despite the lack of a public landing, the bass fishing somehow was famous in the community and there were people who came there to fish even though it was private property.

We were pretty poor. I was writing a novel. My wife, Karen Fonde, was studying to become a teacher. We earned money by working on the farm, which belongs to a college friend. In the winter, we trimmed grapevines for 13 cents a vine. We bundled in heavy clothes and boots and worked even when it was snowing. When the temp got to 10 degrees above, we'd quit and go sit by our wood cook stove. I read War and Peace on breaks from trimming grapes.

Trimming grapevines was no way to get rich. I had no way to buy a boat, fix up a boat, whatever.

But I did have a burning desire to own a boat. I dreamed of having my own sailboat, but that was way out of reach. Then I heard about Jerry's extra boat.

I was in my late twenties, and Jerry seemed pretty old. I guess he was living on Social Security, so he was at least 65. Not really that old, it seems to me now, but now I'm 25 years older myself. Anyway, Jerry was this fellow who had his meager pension checks and lived in a tiny concrete block house on the farm. His little concrete oblong had two rooms. One had a sink with running water from a well, a table, but most of it was filled with a chest freezer. Beyond that was a bedroom.

The freezer was full of fish. Jerry caught the fish. Jerry went fishing every day, no matter the weather. Jerry didn't bother buying a fishing license. Why buy a license when you didn't plan to observe the catch limits, anyway? Jerry used to be hauled into court once in a while to pay fines for poaching fish. He'd say those conservation officers were like ghosts, they were so quiet, and suddenly, there they were asking for his license.

I saw Jerry once fishing on Popendick. He was standing in the bow of a flat-bottomed boat propelled with an electric motor. It was moving slowly and silently while Jerry and a friend played their flies along the surface. This was not the kind of stream fly fishing you see in the sporting magazines and movies. These guys didn't frequent those pricey fly fishing emporia where they will sell you a reel for a thousand bucks. I guess their equipment came from Sears or K-Mart. Or maybe a flea market.

They caught lots of fish. The technique was not that dramatic wrist snapping play that sends a line soaring down a creek to land 60 or 100 feet away, tantalizing a lurking trout. These guys were making their flies flit in little orbiting patterns in a small area over the lake surface. These were working fly fishermen, not sportsmen. They lived off what they caught. Fishing was a job.

It turned out that Jerry owned another boat. It was sitting upside down by a barn. He wanted ten bucks for it.

Ten bucks!

Even I could manage that. Following normal procedures, I sold myself on the boat first, then went for a look. It was a steel boat about 14 feet long. Flat bottom pretty well banged up, as were the sides. I took note of several small holes in the bottom. Liquid Steel would fix that, I thought.

I gave Jerry the ten bucks. I loaded the boat on a wagon and used a tractor to tow it down to Popendick Lake. There I applied Liquid Steel. I let it dry overnight, then launched it. Darned if it didn't float.

Yes, I broke down and bought a pair of oars, so my total outlay was probably around twenty bucks. I didn't bother with a watercraft registration. I mean, this was a private lake, so I figured this would be a private boat. Maybe that was a mistake.

We went fishing in that boat, but soon I discovered some sort of hydraulic principle that says if water comes in contact with Liquid Steel, the Liquid Steel will give. Yes, it will. It tends to happen when you're at the middle of the lake. I bailed with a tin can.. Fish a while, bail a while. I wasn't catching many fish, so it didn't matter.

Back on shore, I'd turn the boat over and dab more Liquid Steel into the holes.

One day I found hundreds of bluegill scales on the bottom of the boat. I was outraged. Somebody had used my boat's bottom as a board to clean fish. They had managed to re-arrange the Liquid Steel, and my leaks were a bit worse that day.

Worse yet, I sensed that the boat had been put in the water. Yes, somebody had taken to "borrowing" it. The nerve!

That day turned into night, nearly, before I rowed back to shore. The moon was over the trees and it was almost dark. I hadn't caught any fish, so all I had to do was pull the boat onto shore and turn it over. As I flipped the boat, I heard a whirring noise and something landed in a tree right over my head.

Hoot!

Spooked me. I grabbed my fishing pole and worms and strode quickly up the lane. A whirring again and there was that owl, again in a branch right over my head.

This time, I trotted down the lane. I'd made it about 30 feet when the owl buzzed me again. That did it. I sprinted all the way out of the woods.

Next time I went to the boat, I forgot to take Liquid Steel along.

Oh well, I thought. I'll go fishing for just a short while.

I learned something more about hydraulics that time. I wasn't too far from shore when a main plug of Liquid Steel popped loose and suddenly I had a gusher. At first I tried my two-handed fishing and bailing. But soon I was bailing steadily. Forget the fish. The water was defeating me. The bottom of the boat had about three inches sloshing around if I stayed level. But I shifted my weight to one side, and suddenly all that water ran to the downhill side. The boat rolled. I shifted my weight towards the other side. It rolled that way and nearly capsized.

This was serious. Sitting as straight as I could, I rowed towards shore, stopped to bail, rowed some more. Soon, water was gaining, so I just rowed and rowed. This was scary. I would look down at the water, and it was so black and deep. Not my friend, this lake. Man, I thought, what would happen if this boat went down? Would it suck me under with it? I had the willies. It was worse than the owl. I rowed and rowed, water sloshed and more than once the boat nearly went on its side.

Finally, I jammed the bow onto the shore and jumped out.

I bailed the boat out, turned it upside down and went home.

What a relief to be on dry land!

A week or so later, I brought a big tube of Liquid Steel down to Popendick.

My boat was gone. Vanished.

Now, I can only imagine one thing happening. This was not a boat anybody would steal. I mean, anyone would be crazy to pay for such a boat, let alone hijack it.

Once again, somebody had "borrowed" my boat.

I hope they could "swim."

NUMBERS GAME

The clerk laid a paper on the counter, and I started writing a check. Wait a minute! There was a long, long number preceded by an X on the registration I was taking out for Plug Nickel.

"What's this?" I said.

"That's your hull number," the Secretary of State clerk said. "You have to have a hull number."

"But I already HAVE a hull number!" I said

True enough. I'd entered the office knowing full well that as far as the International Lightning Class Association was concerned, Plug Nickel was Lightning hull # 9900 and that was an end of it. But not for me was there an end. I had not decided whether nine-nine-oh-oh was going to go on my boat's centerboard trunk. So I equivocated when the clerk asked me about the number.

"There is a number," I said, "But I'm not certain about it."

So what was I doing at the SOS office?

While I was not sure about what number I wanted for the boat, I was quite certain that I wanted a Michigan watercraft license. I'd arranged for a freehand sign man to paint "Plug Nickel" on the boat's stern. While he was at it, I wanted him to paint the registration numbers on the bow. I hate those hardware store decals, you see. So I needed to know, definitely, what the MC numbers were. And to get MC numbers, I needed to register the boat. So there I was, certain about one thing, unclear about another.

What was my problem?

Background: Plug Nickel was built in November 1965 by Dave Nickels. It was the last production wood boat manufactured by Nickels & Holman in the Fenton, Mich. plant now occupied by Nickels Boat Works. Nickels & Holman never sold the hull, never launched it. It was used as a male mold, or plug, for making the female molds which would produce hundreds of Nickels & Holman fiberglass hulls.

When I bought the hull from Dave and George Nickels in November 1994, the brothers told me there was a hull number I could have free. Nine thousand nine hundred. It would not only save me the $100 fee to ILCA, but it would fit roughly with the class chronology, since 9900 would have been issued in the same period when the plug was made.

It would be historically correct.

I equivocated then, too. Sure, historical correctness is fine. I like history as much as the next person. But I planned to restore that hull and equip it with the latest hardware and rigging scheme. What sense did it make to use a tired old number when I was going to have a nimble new boat? Forget nine-nine-zero-zero. I sent a $100 check to the ILCA and asked that they credit me with paying for a number but wait to issue it until my boat was ready to launch (of course, it never occurred to me that it would take more than six years for my boat to be ready for water). I wanted the latest number possible.

At the time, if I'd finished the project when fantasy said it would be done, I'd have gotten a number somewhat shy of 15000. High 14000s sounded great. Wouldn't my friends at Pontiac Yacht Club be amazed to see my pristine sails sporting a high number suspended over my old wooden hull?

As the project took longer and longer, 15000 looked like a possibility. No, I didn't slow my work schedule to achieve a higher number. I had plenty of other pressures holding me back.

A couple years ago, I noticed not so much a switch in thinking as a kind of drift in my thoughts. Maybe it would be better to have the number reflect my boat's true time of creation. I began to regard the ILCA hull number as a sort of birth certificate. Although my boat never was issued a certificate when it was built, 9900 was the closest approximation I would ever have. I asked Karen Johnson at the ILCA about 9900. She checked with Dave Nickels, who assured her no boat ever was issued that number. Karen wanted to be sure no second 9900 would ever appear to confound association records. It was a number paid for but never issued, Dave said. A blank number. With the number approved, I ordered twice times the four digits and filed my new sail numbers away.

> But my son, Abe, is on the other side. Abe is a mathematician. Since he was a toddler, we've called him "Mr. Precise," so I wasn't surprised when he said he'd like the boat to have a number corresponding to when it was made.

Those numbers are still in my file cabinet. Time marched on, and finally, this winter of 2001, the boat is almost finished. That modern hardware set-up is complete. Seats are varnished and screwed tight, floorboards ready to fasten down.

I started getting advice about the number. Bob Mathers, a friend and PYC member who encouraged me to buy the hull back in '94, urged me to drop 9900 and go for a 15000-plus number. Bob is a broker of Lightnings and a fine judge of their value. "Right now, you aren't thinking about selling the plug, but if you ever want to move it, a high sail number could make a $2,000 difference in the price," Bob said.

I mentioned my dilemma to Joe Dissette, who's been sailing Lightnings since the year I was born and dealing them for nearly as long. "The number won't affect the value," said Joe. "It's a wooden boat and everyone knows it."

After all these Flashes columns, how could anybody not know it?

I mentioned the issue to my wife, Karen Fonde. Karen agrees with Bob – the high number would look neat over the old hull, she thinks. But my son, Abe, is on the other side. Abe is a mathematician. Since he was a toddler, we've called him "Mr. Precise," so I wasn't surprised when he said he'd like the boat to have a number corresponding to when it was made.

So there I stood at the Secretary of State counter with a registration bearing that godawful long number with an X in front. I'd need two sails to hold those digits. No way. Problem was that I had no way of instantly acquiring a new 15000-plus number. No way could I call Karen at the ILCA and spring a number.

It occurred to me that whatever value my boat has will not be based on the amount of money I've invested in such accoutrements as oval aluminum spars and new Harken hardware. Here's why:

Recently, I was invited by the ILCA to display Plug Nickel at the June 16-17 Designer Recognition Rendezvous at Mystic Seaport in honor of Sparkman & Stephens, who designed the Lightning and many other neat boats. The show is sponsored in part by Mystic Seaport Museum and WoodenBoat Magazine. Why me? Not because of my boat's state-of-the-art rig. It's because of what Plug Nickel embodies – that precise point in the history of Lightning sailboats when a major boat builder abandoned wood construction and adopted the new fiberglass medium. Plug Nickel's hull and deck are the progenitor of all those Nickels & Holman glass boats.

The clerk was waiting for me to make up my mind.

"Make it Ninety-Nine-Hundred," I said.

BOOM TIME

One Sunday in April. My alarm went off at 6 a.m. and as I clambered out of bed, I checked down a mental list of things to do on my wooden Lightning. For once, there was nothing, zero, on the list.

The previous weekend, I'd spent the better part of a Saturday in the company of Dave Nickels as he salvaged the oval aluminum mast I'd bought ages ago for use on Plug Nickel.

I'd bought two oval masts from people in Kansas whose Lightning was vandalized. Someone built a fire under it. They sold me all that was left – sails, rudder, spinnaker pole, hardware and, for some reason I've forgotten, not one but two masts.

I had the two masts trucked from Kansas. One day I came home to find two black metal posts lying on my driveway. I loaded them on a boat trailer and left them at Nickels Boat Works in Fenton, Mich. Memory grows dim on projects like this, but I believe that was five, maybe even six years ago.

Back in January, I'd booked Saturday, March 31, as my time to work with Dave Nickels to make sure the better of the two masts would fit my "new" Lightning. When I arrived, I found Dave had hauled both masts out and had chosen the better of the pair for me.

Modern rig for a classic boat: Spinnaker blocks and bridle hardware in place.

But we were not quite ready to put it in the boat. Some hardware was missing. To replace it, we needed to remove fragments of foam the manufacturer had placed in the mast in hopes that it would float in case of a capsize. That foam had disintegrated, and it took the better part of the morning just to rid the mast of the last chunks. No way could we maneuver cables and ropes through the mast with pieces of foam lying in the way.

By the end of the day, on Dave's orders, I stood back and watched him raise the mast and place it in the plug, a job that takes two people when I do it. Now I had a fully rigged modern mast for my wooden boat.

But wasn't I forgetting something?

Well, yes. My boat was not quite ready to be launched that Sunday in early April. I would still need a boom.

Of course, if I wanted to launch it with one of my wooden masts, I could sail with a wooden boom. But I was intent on launching it with the metal spars, as I'd always planned. Besides, the wooden mast and boom are another story. Please, don't let me digress.

Hah! Plug Nickel IS a digression, is it not? Isn't that the wonder of these boat projects? Who really needs them? They are digressions, sidepaths through life.

But hey, back to the boom.

Nickels Boat Works had one for me. Did I want them to rig it, or just have them sell me a kit of parts and do it myself?

Do any readers not know the answer to that question?

Had I not rigged this entire boat myself? How difficult could it be to put a boom together? Work of an hour or two, at most.

So one morning early, before work, I tooled on up to Fenton to pick up a blank boom tube and the parts kit.

The kit wasn't ready, and I watched as Dave went about assembling a set of parts for a boom that was to have the mainsheet run inside. That is trickier than having blocks hanging underneath and outside the boom. Good thing the parts weren't ready. There are lots of pieces to this internal block puzzle, and they have to be put together in sequence, or it won't work.

I gathered that the key thing was to have a long stick with screws on both ends and a jam cleat on one end so you can stretch the entire outhaul system – rope, wire, block and shackle

– in a line inside the boom. All parts will then be lying under the holes where they need to be mounted on the boom. But you have to be careful to mount blocks and thimble sleeve before riveting the front boom casting and outhaul casting in place. Do it out of sequence, and you'll be trapped outside the boom.

Dave measured and inked in the places where I would need to drill holes. It all looked straightforward enough as Dave talked me through the procedure. I recall being tempted to go home and put it together right then.

But I didn't. I put the boom and box of parts in my minivan and headed south for my office.

Two days later, I set out my parts. I built my assembly stick. The boom seemed dirty, so I cleaned it inside with detergent. Outside, I rubbed it with acetone, making it shine.

Only then did I notice that I'd scrubbed off those ink marks Dave made to show me where to drill the holes. Uh-oh. Undeterred, I pulled out his step-by-step instructions.

What was this? It looked like code: Harken part numbers, but I was unsure which was which.

I sure wished I had not rubbed those marks off.

Did I really want to drill holes in this immaculate metal tube and then find that I'd put them in the wrong spot?

I filled a few mistaken holes on the boat, but this is metal. A wrong hole could cause problems.

I began to see a very bad day ahead – wrong holes and

Sign painter Dave Varga gives my boat a name.

many frustrations, because this was a do-it-right-the-first-time project.

It was still early on a Saturday morning. I made a call to Fenton. What, I asked, would it take for someone at Nickels to assemble this boom?

"About 45 minutes," said Dave Nickels.
The drive to Fenton is also 45 minutes.
I was on the road.

PLUG IT IN

I was leaning over the stern of my boat in a light wind, coasting slowly past a small island in the western end of Cass Lake. The rudder was grinding against the shallow bottom, and my imagination filled with horrible outcomes: Gudgeons torn out of transoms, or entire sterns yanked galley west.

In a few seconds, I popped the rudder out of its gudgeons and began steering by trimming sails. As I yanked the rudder, I couldn't help reading – upside down – the tall script letters I'd had painted there:

Plug Nickel.

Suddenly, it was real. The hull that had lain stationary for so many years finally was a boat, moving in three dimensions. A real sailboat subject to all the dangers any boat may face. And now we were sailing in it without a rudder, moving toward deeper water.

It was May 4, 2001, and finally I was sailing my wooden Lightning whose hull I bought in November 1994. Nearly seven years of fussing, scraping, pounding, hours spent on my back in the bow or bent over a drill making holes in the deck and at last it was in the water nearly 36 years after Dave Nickels built it.

It seemed unreal. Here I was sitting on the deck that wiggled, pitched and rolled like a real sailboat after hundreds of hours of static time messing with it on a trailer in my shop.

May 4 was not the real launch. That happened on Saturday, April 28, late in a warm, still afternoon. Together with a few friends and family, I'd shipped the mast and backed it down to the boat launch at Pontiac Yacht Club. There had been some tense moments with the beginnings of a real headache as I lay, once again, under the deck, trying to puzzle how to fit the mast into its shoe.

Bob Mathers, an old hand at this, pointed out that the mast could slide in its shoe. I was trying to make it fit tightly between the shoe's two bolts, and it could not work that way. Relieved of that worry, my headache wondrously vanished, and I hauled the boat in a wide arc to avoid branches on the club's big hardwood trees.

Earlier, Bob had helped me install a red spar fly on the top of the mast. But my arc was not wide enough and once again, a spar fly bit the dust. A record for me – wind indicator knocked down two hours after installation, and the boat so far not even in the water.

The big moment came. I backed the trailer into the water, and in the mirror I watched Plug Nickel float free.

Jumping aboard, I pulled off my nondescript T-shirt and scrambled into the one that had lain for years at the bottom of a drawer in our bedroom.

"Thank God It Floats."

And it did float!

Despite a tiny trickle of water coming in through the bailer, the boat was riding very high.

Bob Mathers reported the skeg was hardly in the water. "The boat is light, maybe 680 pounds."

After pouring some champagne on the deck, my son, Abe, and old sailing buddy Wylie Gerdes and I took our places and hoisted main and jib. There was no wind, yet Plug Nickel moved sedately down bay. We tacked, and sailed slowly back to shore.

"What do you think of it?" Wylie asked.

"It's a boat," I said.

Frankly, I was in shock. Numb.

Boat restoration is a mental state. The process of making this vessel ready to launch had taken so long that it had become a mental way of life. It was hard to process the fact that this boat was no longer sitting on a trailer in a dimly lit building waiting for me to commit the next snafu of hardware placement. It had survived all that and was now in the water.

But as a boat, a true floating craft, it is not beyond my ability to commit the next gaffe. It is subject to all the dangers any boat faces.

So it was that day when Wylie and I were sailing without a

rudder. As soon as we reached deep water, I leaned over the stern and held the rudder vertically in the water. It wanted to bob away from me, but we were not moving fast and I managed to slip the pintles into the gudgeons.

It was a good rehearsal. Two days later, Abe and my wife, Karen Fonde, and I were sailing through whitecaps on a windy Sunday afternoon. I was pleased to see that water was no longer coming in through the bailer.

My fine reverie was interrupted as I noticed a tugging on the tiller and realized I'd placed the stick on top of the bridle rig rather than underneath. Strain from the mainsail was pressing the bridle cables upward against the tiller, which, being of modern design, does not swivel up and down. Suddenly, the tiller was free, and so was the rudder – it had been lifted clean out of the gudgeons and was trailing on its side behind the boat.

Wind was 15-20 m.p.h. and we were on a course for shore. I let the main out, shouted for Abe to let out jib, and we pointed away from land. I leaned over the transom to re-set the rudder. Unlike the other day, there was real hard pressure on the blade as I tried to hold it straight and guide the pintles into the gudgeons. We were racing fast through the water. The rudder would slant off to the side. I tried once. No good. Tried again. No way. We seemed to be moving even faster.

I should mention that my normal rudder, the illegal kickup rudder, is in California, where my older son, Adam, is building two replicas – a nice new Honduran mahogany kickup rudder for Plug Nickel and a second rudder to sell.

That's why I was in this jam, because not only does the kickup rudder fold up when it meets the lake bottom, but also the tiller pivots up and down and would simply have moved out of the way if pressured by nearby cables.

I kept telling myself, I did this two days ago. Yes, there was less wind. But I KNOW it can be done.

I pushed very hard to keep the rudder in the vertical plane. Lower pintle just barely into the gudgeon. Water rushing hard around it. Pushing hard, I moved the upper, shorter, pintle above the little hole and pushed down.

Whew! Rudder in, and we could steer.

For a moment, I was afraid I'd ram my nice new boat into somebody's dock.

My nice new boat. Yes, it's a real boat.

THE CARETAKER

Nothing whets a collector's appetite more than hearing that the first unit – Serial Number One – of some old product is still around. When I heard that Lightning # 1 would be on display at Mystic Seaport the weekend of June 15-17, 2001, I got pretty excited. I'd already agreed to be there myself, showing Plug Nickel, my Lightning # 9900. But the sight of this old boat, Number One, with the light green deck and cracked transom, was the highlight of the show. By Sunday, ILCA President Mary Huntsman, her husband Sandy and ILCA Secretary Karen Johnson had worked out a deal whereby the association will "buy" Lightning #1 and "loan" it to Mystic Seaport Museum.

#1 on show at Mystic

It was a happy outcome for Number One. But it could have been different. There was a time when an owner was desperate to rid himself of the old woodie and its ritual upkeep. Nobody – not the Smithsonian, not the town of Skaneateles where it was made, even – wanted to buy the boat. For many artifacts, that is the critical fork in the road. Does it go to the landfill, or will someone step forward and take responsibility for it?

This is how Lightning # 1 was saved.

Summer of 1971. An FBI agent from the bureau's Utica, New York office jumps into one of New York's Finger Lakes and swims out to a sad sack wooden sailboat moored offshore.

What's he looking for?

Was this part of some big drug sting or white collar crime investigation?

Truth is that jack Ryan, then 33, couldn't have explained even to himself why he was splashing toward that woebegone sailboat.

Because it was for sale?

But Ryan already had a sailboat. It was a wooden Lightning, # 754, made by the Skaneateles Boat Co. ion Skaneateles, New York.

"Most beautiful I'd ever seen in my life," Ryan told me.

Jack Ryan rigging #1

The summer before, Ryan had discovered the immaculate Lightning. When he saw it, he traded his power boat for the Lightning and went sailing. By spring of 1971, he was sailing Lightning 754 at Oneida lake. What more did he need? He had a fine looking, great sailing classic boat.

One day, he visited another of the Finger lakes. At a boat club on Cazenovia Lake, someone pointed to a bulletin board. A 3-by-5 card noted that the first Lightning ever built was for sale.

$1,500 for boat, trailer, sails, cover.

Urged by his wife and kids to go have a look, Ryan drove to the seller's house. That's all he wanted to do, Ryan says. Just see what the first Lightning looked like.

Problem was, the boat was moored. 30 yards offshore. The owner wanted badly to sell it, though, so he lent Ryan swimming trunks.

No tender. It was swim or go home.

Back in the car, his wife and kids were waiting for him to go see

Cockpit of Lightning #1 during Sunday rainstorm with 2 inches of water in bottom. Note the belaying pins and brass winch forward.

the boat.

"I'm upset at my wife for getting me into this," Ryan said.

As Ryan and the owner, Hume Laidman, were paddling out to the boat, Laidman said, "I'm asking fifteen hundred, and I'll take twelve."

Ryan, not the greatest swimmer, didn't answer. He looked at the boat. "It was a mess. It was awful. The cover was almost rotted. It was dirty. There was water in the bottom, plus six inches of leaves."

Somehow, all these negatives turned Ryan's head.

"I'm interested," Ryan said. Why? It was Number One.

"I wanted to buy it right then, but he insisted I come back and sail it before I buy it."

A few days later, Ryan went back. The boat had been spruced up, but it was still dirty. It didn't matter. Ryan had a plan.

That winter, Ryan's car stayed outside. In the garage, he sanded the hull. Originally, he knew, the hull was painted white and the deck was green. By the time Ryan got it, someone had painted it red, white and blue. Ryan removed all the paint, took off the canvas which was cracked.

"I put every screw in a bucket, which was stupid – every screw as a different size."

"I had fun tearing it to pieces."

Ryan re-painted it red, white and blue. He left the inside of the hull gray.

He noticed oddities, the sort of inconsistencies consistent with a prototype. The cockpit coaming on one side is 3/4 inch deeper than on the other. Floorboards have notches cut in them, as if they were made out of remnants from some other project.

When it was built in 1938, #1 had no skeg. Ryan eventually put a skeg on it to make it conform to class rules. He didn't notice any difference in the way it sailed, with or without the skeg.

Over time, Ryan learned his boat's history. The first owner was Gordon Cronk, who bought it the same day Skaneateles took the first publicity photos of its new product. Number One was shown wailing without a rudder, steering by trimming sails.

The second owner, Lou Ayres, eventually had the centerboard trunk rebuilt and covered the bottom with fiberglass. It was leaking.

He also documented the boat's history. He acquired negatives of old Skaneateles Boat Co. publicity photos for Number One.

I asked Ryan if there was a drain plug, and he laughed. "The centerboard trunk!"

If the water leaks in through the trunk, it can go back that way.

A previous owner installed a motor well, but Ryan covered it.

Ryan has re-finished the boat three times. He found that the deck is plywood, not planked like later production boats.

Hume Laidman was desperate to sell the boat in 1971. "He didn't want to put it away again," Ryan said.

Laidman had contacted the Smithsonian.

"They showed a great deal of interest, but as a donation," said Ryan.

Laidman contacted the city of Skaneateles to see if they wanted to buy the first edition of the boat that made their town famous among sailors.

"They wanted to buy it, but he wanted $1,500. $1,500! Who did he think he was?"

Laidman put modern hardware on the boat. Ryan removed the new stuff and gradually added vintage bronze pieces. The boat has its original belaying pins in the pin rack behind the mast. There is a big round bronze winch for holding the jib sheets. Lines and sheets are manilla hemp, though he couldn't get hemp of the quality available in the 1930s.

In 1972, Ryan took # 1 to the Thousand Islands Antique Boat Show in Clayton, New York. It was mainly a power boat show. He was told he could leave it on display for a time, but "get it out of the way when the nice boats come."

One of the judges was Howard Chapelle, boatbuilding historian from the Smithsonian Institution. Another was Moulton Farnham, editor of Small Boat Journal.

The judges ruled Lightning # 1 classic boat of the year.

"We didn't leave that spot when the fancy boats came," laughed

Ryan.

Ryan came to Mystic last week with one goal: he didn't want to take # 1 back home to Peoria, Illinois. What he wanted was a commitment to pay him $25,000 for the boat.

Sunday afternoon, Ryan hit the road for Peoria.

Number One still sat where he rigged it. A hard, long rain was coming down and there was a good two inches of water in the bottom. Underneath, you could see water dripping out.

Through the centerboard trunk.

Lighting Number One won't be leaving Mystic.

It **is** the fancy boat.

MAYBE

15 1/2-foot SNIPE sailboat w/sails, trailer, $300.

So read the classified ad in the South Bend Tribune.

It was 1982. I was working for the Tribune as a reporter in the paper's Cass County, Michigan news Bureau. The "bureau" was a spare room in the winterized porch of our house in the village of Marcellus about 30 miles south of Kalamazoo, ditto west of Three Rivers and a little less than that east of Dowagiac. Middle of nowheresville, in other words.

According to the 1980 census, Marcellus had 1,134 inhabitants. Human inhabitants. Standing in the back yard in the winter, I could hear cows mooing, and in the summer from the space place I could smell the perfume of pigs. A small town, though with several bars and VFW hall, you couldn't say there wasn't action – if you were into drinking and fighting.

Otherwise, well, I guess you could say I was spoiling for a project. And the ad implied that if I ought this Snipe, my project would be sailing.

In a boat like the one I learned to sail in as a kid. That was at Camp Manitoulin, on Barlow Lake near Middleville, Michigan. It was a two-week course and it was pretty though, given that we were 10-year-olds with no sailing experience. Although in my case, I had some sailing background – I'd read novels about the sea and could have come at it from a romantic angle. Could have, except that as I said, the class was pretty tough and there was no time for daydreaming.

There was time in class with an instructor drawing wind angles and little triangular sails on a blackboard, and there was time on the water, swimming out to the boat, learning about clew outhauls and heads and tacks and centerboards and how to read the water for wind and steer a straight course using a point on land and bring the boat back to a buoy, etc.

That was in the mid-1950s. I went home elated that I had acquired the skill, or at least semi-skill, of sailing. But at home, there was no interest in sailing. It was not that there was no interest in boats. There was. But my father, who was a pilot in World War II and flew fast airplanes, was a motor kind of guy. And so, after he finished building our house, he looked upon the leftover oak floor boards and, being a designer of stores, sat down and drew plans for a 17-foot runabout.

I watched him build it in the garage of our new house. And it was while observing as he cut and assembled those boards into frames as a boat-like skeleton emerged that I understood the true purpose of a garage.

A garage is a place to build a boat.

Or, it would turn out, to fix one, although nowadays we're so fancy we say we're "restoring" the boat.

It happened in those days at Marcellus that we were renting one of the biggest houses in town. It was truly imposing, a large, box-like two-story house with four big bedrooms upstairs, a large living room and dining room, and a porch with insulated windows where I could set a desk, typewriter, primitive computer, phone and where I could work as a newspaper reporter.

Almost forgot. There was a garage.

It was while sitting cross-legged on the floor, clipping and filing news stories, that I ran across the ad.

A Snipe! Images of those happy days at Camp Manitoulin flashed through my brain. Blackened troughs of wavelets as a line squall moved in front of our boat. The quick pitch of the hull as the main and jib filled and we hiked out from the deck.

$300! Practically a gift.

Located somewhere in Niles, not too far from Marcellus.

I called the owner, made an appointment and had a look.

"It's perfectly sailable," they guy said.

The trailer was heavy, a homemade job with big car tires. The bearings were nearly shot, but I didn't know that then.

The boat had a blue hull and white deck. The deck looked iffy, but I questioned the black stuff around the frames on the bottom of the hull, inside. It was hard material of some kind.

It hose days, my dad was traveling around the state as a

drugstore designer. He happened to be going to Niles, so I asked him to stop and look at the Snipe.

"Don't buy it," he warned me. "Somebody put tar in the bottom."

His reasoning: Tar meant the owner was trying to stop leaks from the inside. Somewhere, there had to be rot. Stay away.

So I drove down to Niles and bought the boat.

I already had a name for it.

To my wife I said, "Maybe it'll float, maybe it'll sink."

"I'll call it 'maybe.'"

That was in the month of October. Late October.

What first appeared to be tar was some kind of plastic resin. I never learned why it was put there. Eventually, I would sand it off. The boat was carvel-planked, meaning it had broad cedar planks on wooden frames that may or may not have been oak. The deck was made of plywood. The mast and boom were spruce and very pretty.

It was November 4 when I launched Maybe Cold enough for sweaters and long pants. I took Maybe to Cedar Lake a few miles north of Marcellus. There's a state boat launch on a little cove hemmed in by lily pads. The lilies were a real navigational hazard, I would find.

My crew was an old friend, Danny Willbach, visiting from new York. He'd done a little sailing and volunteered to go out with me so long as his new shoes didn't get wet. I said fine, get in.

I raised the main sail and the boat began to move directly towards the lily pads. This was my first experience with a rigid rudder since Manitoulin days. The little glass boat I was used to sailing has a kick-up rudder. While I was waiting for the boat to go into water deep enough to ship the rudder, the wind drove me into those lily pads and toward several tall trees on shore. I leaped out of the boat into the lilies, soaking my pants and sweater. Treading on all that vegetation, I tried to interpose my strength against the wind as it forced the hull across the green pads and smack against the shore with the sail snagged in a tree.

From his perch in the cockpit, Danny watched. He couldn't do much because of his shoes. I waded chest-high around the hull, grabbed the painter and hauled the boat away from shore and those offending trees. Then I grabbed the edge of the cockpit and pulled myself aboard.

There was some question now about Danny's shoes, though, because I noticed the aft end of the centerboard trunk was spouting water like a faucet. The cockpit would soon be a dangerous place for fancy shoes.

The danger of being too close to shore without a rudder is that you can bang into trees. The danger of being away from shore without a rudder is that you might not get back, trees or no trees. Despite all that training at Camp Manitoulin, I could not seem to make the boat sail. Rather, I couldn't make it sail ahead. We were moving, but backwards. I seemed to be perpetually in irons. I kept trying to make the boat come about. The air was light, though, and I had to skull with the rudder. I tried to dredge up memories of those blackboard sketches back at Manitoulin. Where was the wind? Should I tighten or loosen the sail? But even on a new tack, Maybe wouldn't sail.

Now what had appeared from the landing as the opposite shore was turning out to be the shore close by. My family – my wife and two young sons – were little dots on the other side of the lake.

This was not fun. I was in a sailboat, and there was wind. There was also water being pumped into my boat through some circuitous hydrological path in the centerboard trunk. I was moving backwards, slowly. And I was humiliated as my wife and kids watched from shore and a fisherman at anchor seemed to race past me.

To this point, I'd been vigorously active, coming about, or at least trying to point the boat in one and then another direction. Finally, I took my hand off the tiller. I watched as the boat pivoted slowly and the sails filled. Without any steering from me, Maybe had found the wind and was moving slowly ahead. I left the tiller alone. We picked up speed. Now I put my hand on the tiller and held the course Maybe had found.

As we moved ahead, I noticed that water was no longer pumping out of the centerboard trunk. I felt a strong pull from the mainsheet and the hull hiked to the side. We scrambled up high and I looked down the length of that white deck.

Wow! We were sailing, and this was my boat!

I looked closer at the deck and for the first time noticed cracks. Somehow, I'd have to fix that.

But meanwhile, what a discovery: Even if I could not, my Snipe knew how to sail.

Most wonderful of all, Danny's shoes were dry!

THE PESSIMIST

If you want to fix up old boats, you really should be a pessimist.

If somebody offers you a worn-out 1953 Snipe, sails and trailer for $300, don't fantasize yourself onto some idyllic lake with white sails billowing overhead. Don't whoop for joy and peel off the 100-dollar bills. Think about why the boat is priced so cheaply and make a lowball counter-offer.

Nothing, zero, nada would be a good price to offer.

If the seller declines, walk away. Be sure of one thing – there is another junker boat out there waiting for your time, energy and money.

Just like I did, right?

Well, okay, when it comes to boats and pessimism, I have a real battle. If we used the analogy of the glass half full, I'd be a hull half-full kind of guy.

Half full of water, unfortunately.

I sure would like to be a pessimist. I'm the guy who paid $300 for that dilapidated Snipe. I never kept track of how much money I sunk in polyester resin, fiberglass fabric, wood, screws and tools to turn that hull into a working sailboat.

Did I enjoy the project?

Oh, yes.

Did I enjoy sailing the boat?

For a time, until I got too busy with fixing my second loser Snipe.

That one only cost $150.

It didn't have a trailer, but I rationalized that the hull was in better shape. It only needed to be sanded and scraped, oh yes, have its deck replaced.

Only.

I'm good at being a pessimist about other people's boats.

My friend Josh told me last month about the Catalina 22 sailboat he was offered for $1,500 with an outboard motor and trailer, sails, the works. How could he walk away from that? An outboard motor! A trailer!

What a deal, I thought. And I had a second thought: He'll never sail it this year.

I saw Josh and his dad last weekend as they embarked on major fiberglass repairs to the hull and deck. Not to mention the broken mast.

What a deal.

Here's a good thing to remember: Trailers and outboard motors don't help a boat to float.

After investing huge amounts of time and money in that Catalina, Josh scrapped the boat.

I was right in the beginning, but who am I to talk?

I found that second Snipe upside-down behind the Diamond lake yacht Club at Cassopolis, Michigan. That was about 1984. I don't recall how I got it back to our house in Marcellus. We had a barn behind our house, and I stowed the boat there and began scraping paint off the bottom. At the time, I was a reporter with the South bend Tribune.

Actually, I was chief of the Tribune's Cass County News Bureau. I didn't know about that promotion until I was about the leave the paper. The bureau was a spare bedroom in our house with a phone listed to the paper and a computer that was antiquated even by early 1980s standards. I was the only reporter in the bureau. As chief, I suppose my subordinates were our golden retriever, Jessie, and out cat, Sancho Panza. I learned of my chiefhood one day when I made a rare appearance in South Bend and asked the librarian for a file photo of me. I needed it in my job search. On the back of the photo the label said, "Joel Thurtell, Cass County Bureau Chief."

If I'd been really savvy, I'd have demanded a raise on the spot.

Instead, I went home and scraped the bottom of a wooden sailboat.

By fall of 1984, I had a job offer from the Detroit Free Press. Lo and behold, the Free Press was going to pay my moving expenses. One day in early 1985, after we bought our first house in Plymouth, a Bekins moving can backed up to our Marcellus house to begin loading furniture. They workers had filled the first half of the trailer when I told them to stop. As I'd hoped, there was space enough left for guess what: The Snipe hull.

That boat fit perfectly inside the garage of our house in Plymouth. What are garages for? Later. I drove across the state to Marcellus and trailed my first Snipe, Maybe, to its new home.

Now I had two boats – one to sail and one to play with.

Odd way to put it: Sail one and play with the other sounds like sailing, the supposed recreation, is the work, while fixing a boat, which is real work, is play.

Of course, the more overwhelming aspect of that playing-fixing up thing is the money it costs. Once again, I was buying wood, screws, resin, fabric and more tools.

I recall buying two sheets of what I was told was marine-grade plywood for the deck. The dimensions of a Snipe deck are such that one 4-foot-by-8-foot sheet of plywood will make one side of the deck. The previous owner had "rolled" the cockpit sides of the deck, which means he had rounded the frames, curving them downward as they sloped inward. Easier on the butt for sailors, but hard to make plywood conform to the radical curve. As I say, one side was very had to bend, the other side was easier. I thought nothing of it at the time.

By the time I launched the news Snipe, also known as Maybe, I had sold the first Maybe. The new Maybe was great. I varnished the deck and it looked real spiffy.

For a few weeks.

Then, I noticed a change. The surface of the deck was beginning to pull away from the rest of the plywood. I soon learned the word for this: "Delamination."

It only happened on one side of the deck.

It seemed that any exposure to water, as sometimes happens when a boat is placed on a lake, was causing serious decomposition on one side of the deck. The other side still looked great under its several coats of spar varnish.

I realized, eventually, that one of the pieces of supposedly marine-grade plywood was really interior-grade material and couldn't stand exposure to water.

Back to the garage, but this time it sat for several years. We moved to another house, and the boat went into my stall in the new garage.

At the very least, I would have to replace half the deck. But it probably wouldn't match the other half, so I'd want to replace the entire deck. It was hard to contemplate doing the whole job over again.

Why it didn't occur to me to replace half the deck and just paint the whole thing, I don't know. Probably because I really liked how it looked in varnish, I guess.

By this time, I was sailing a glass boat. First, it was a 470, and that turning out to be too small, I made the jump to a glass Lightning, # 11520 by Nickels & Holman.

I was sailing.

Not laboring on boats.

The old Snipe sat upside-down in my side of the two-stall garage.

Under pressure from my supreme adviser, Karen, I offered the boat to a friend, a wooden boat lover and accomplished woodworker.

One day my pal showed up with a makeshift trailer and we loaded the Snipe. I said goodbye.

The price?

Nothing. Zero.

Yes, folks, I gave that boat away.

I never kept books on how much that second maybe cost me. I hate to think. To some it would seem like cheap fun. A grand, maybe.

So I'm certainly a pessimist when it comes to figuring the true cost of boat projects.

But I learn my pessimism slowly.

Early the summer I launched Plug Nickel, I looked into insurance for my "new" boat. AA wouldn't consider it – too old. I talked to a guy at BoatUS who wanted me to have it surveyed. For two or three hundred bucks.

How much do you have into it? He asked.

I bridled at his nosiness.

Okay, for starters, $500 for the hull.

That's on record.

Do I want people to know how much I sunk into that project over seven years?

Do I want my wife to know?

Most of all, do I want to know myself?

Sorry, folks, I'm busy.

I need to call a guy.

He wants me to take his boat.

For free.

About the author

When he was ten, Joel Thurtell learned to sail on a Snipe at a YMCA camp in western Michigan. Many years later, he bought his first wooden boat. It was a 1953 Wagemaker Snipe. He replaced the deck, repaired and painted the hull and sailed his "new" boat happily until he found another wooden Snipe in need of help.

As his two sons grew, Thurtell found that Lightnings were a better fit than the smaller Snipe. For the past eight years, Thurtell has been sailing his restored wooden Lightning, Plug Nickel.

In his spare time, Thurtell was a reporter for the Berrien Springs Journal Era, South Bend Tribune and Detroit Free Press until he retired from newspapers in 2007. Now he sails, works on boats and writes books.

www.ingramcontent.com/pod-product-compliance
Lightning Source LLC
Chambersburg PA
CBHW070311100426
42743CB00011B/2436